T0093428

Advances in Complex Decision Making

The rapidly evolving business and technology landscape demands sophisticated decision-making tools to stay ahead of the curve. *Advances in Complex Decision Making: Using Machine Learning and Tools for Service-Oriented Computing* is a cutting-edge technical guide exploring the latest decision-making technology advancements. This book provides a comprehensive overview of machine learning algorithms and examines their applications in complex decision-making systems in a service-oriented framework.

The authors also delve into service-oriented computing and how it can be used to build complex systems that support decision making. Many real-world examples are discussed in this book to provide a practical insight into how discussed techniques can be applied in various domains, including distributed computing, cloud computing, IoT and other online platforms.

For researchers, students, data scientists and technical practitioners, this book offers a deep dive into the current developments of machine learning algorithms and their applications in service-oriented computing. This book discusses various topics, including Fuzzy Decisions, ELICIT, OWA aggregation, Directed Acyclic Graph, RNN, LSTM, GRU, Type-2 Fuzzy Decision, Evidential Reasoning algorithm and robust optimisation algorithms. This book is essential for anyone interested in the intersection of machine learning and service computing in complex decision-making systems.

Walayat Hussain received his PhD in Computer Science from the University of Technology Sydney, Australia. Currently, he is the Head of the Information Technology Discipline at the PFBS, Australian Catholic University, Australia. His current research interests are cloud/edge computing, business intelligence, decision-support systems, AI and machine learning.

Honghao Gao is currently with the School of Computer Engineering and Science, Shanghai University, China. He is also a professor at the College of Future Industry, Gachon University, Korea. His research interests include software security, cloud/edge computing, intelligent data processing and AI4Healthcare. Prof. Gao is a fellow of the Institution of Engineering and Technology (IET) and a fellow of the British Computer Society (BCS).

Fethi Rabhi received a PhD in Computer Science at the University of Sheffield in 1990. He is a professor at the School of Computer Science and Engineering at the University of New South Wales in Australia, specialising in software engineering applied to Business Applications.

Luis Martínez received MSc and PhD degrees in Computer Sciences, both from the University of Granada, Spain. He is a full professor in the Department of Computer Science at the University of Jaén. His current research interests are fuzzy decision making, fuzzy systems, decision-support systems, computing with words and recommender systems.

Advances in Complex Decision Making

Using Machine Learning and Tools for Service-Oriented Computing

Edited by
Walayat Hussain
Honghao Gao
Fethi Rabhi
Luis Martínez

CRC Press
Taylor & Francis Group
Boca Raton London New York

CRC Press is an imprint of the
Taylor & Francis Group, an **informa** business

A CHAPMAN & HALL BOOK

Designed cover image: © Getty

First edition published 2024
by CRC Press
4 Park Square, Milton Park, Abingdon, Oxon, OX14 4RN

and by CRC Press
2385 Executive Center Drive, Suite 320, Boca Raton, FL 33431

CRC Press is an imprint of Informa UK Limited

British Library Cataloguing-in-Publication Data
A catalogue record for this book is available from the British Library

ISBN: 978-1-032-37527-4 (hbk)
ISBN: 978-1-032-37526-7 (pbk)
ISBN: 978-1-003-34062-1 (ebk)

DOI: 10.1201/9781003340621

Typeset in Times
by SPi Technologies India Pvt Ltd (Straive)

Contents

Preface

Making decision has always been one of the key aspects of our lives, whether we are faced with simple or complex problems. The ability to make an effective decision is essential in various domains, including business, health, education and various other government sectors. With the advent of the advanced computing technologies, such as service-oriented computing and robust machine learning algorithms, complex decision making has become more efficient and accurate than ever before. These technologies provided new tools and methods to analyse large structured and unstructured data and identify complex hidden patterns for informed decision-making processes. In this book, we present a collection of current research work showcasing the latest advances and applications in addressing complex decision-making processes.

This book is intended for students, researchers and practitioners interested in exploring current approaches to using machine learning in service-oriented computing framework to address complex decision-making challenges. This book comprises six chapters from leading experts in the field, including academics and industry research analysts, covering a wide range of topics such as decision making under uncertainty, fuzzy decisions, decision support systems, predictive analytics using deep learning algorithms, natural language processing and others.

Chapter 1, "Application of Choquet–OWA Aggregation Operator to Fuse ELICIT Information", presents that multi-criteria decision-making (MCDM) problems become increasingly complex. Experts have difficulty in quantifying their opinions on each alternative and prefer to express their preference information linguistically. In the existing linguistic representation models, the extended comparative linguistic expressions with the symbolic translation (ELICIT) model stand out due to its powerful ability to express the hesitancy of experts and obtain results with a higher interpretability and accuracy. Given the importance of the aggregation process in the resolution of MCDM problems, the definition of ELICIT aggregation operators has become a research hotspot. Among them, it is the ELICIT ordered weighted aggregation (ELICIT-OWA) operator, since the OWA operator is one of the most classical and popular tools to fuse decision information. However, the weights used in the aggregation are computed from the assumption that the criteria are mutually independent, which may not be realistic in some MCDM problems. In this sense, the Choquet integral does allow for reflecting the interrelationship among elements by means of the definition of a fuzzy measure. Therefore, the chapter proposes a novel ELICIT-OWA operator that calculates weights via Choquet integral, taking full account of the relationships between criteria, in order to obtain a realistic aggregation result. On this basis, a new approach to solving MCDM problems.

Chapter 2, "GPipe: Using Adaptive Directed Acyclic Graphs to Run Data and Feature Pipelines with On-the-Fly Transformations", discusses that businesses can gain significant value from the data for decision making via the construction of complex data analytics pipelines. The approaches have a dual purpose of creating reports and serving Machine Learning (ML) models. These pipelines implement transformations via scripts that read raw data from different sources, aggregate, clean, transform and save it back into tables. The main challenge addressed in this chapter is how to efficiently transform raw data on-the-fly into features to be used by ML models. At the same time, the efforts required to maintain the scripts in the face of changes must be minimised. The chapter proposes a hybrid approach that trades between supporting dependency change management and allowing partial processing while ensuring platform independence. The approach uses a Directed Acyclic Graph (DAG) to represent data and feature transformations to minimise the overall processing required and ease the maintenance of the data processing scripts. The chapter presents a prototype to evaluate the proposed architecture and discusses preliminary performance results.

Chapter 3, "Building an ESG Decision-Making System: Challenges and Research Directions", discusses that several government and international organisations are pushing for the adoption of various Environmental, Social and Governance (ESG) goals. There are many IT-related challenges associated with such changes that require various academic communities to undertake new research studies. The chapter advocates that such ESG-linked changes should be tackled as a multidisciplinary collaboration between different academic disciplines. It categorises new research into three streams – strategising, architecting and developing ESG systems to respond to multiple forces. The chapter then discusses how to design ESG decision-making systems to support ESG goals.

Chapter 4, "Analysing Trust, Security and Cost of Cloud Consumer's Reviews using RNN, LSTM and GRU", discusses that choosing an appropriate cloud provider has always been an essential task for a cloud consumer. Within a cloud paradigm, cloud services are offered by various cloud service providers to fulfil the requirements of service consumers to maintain a trustful relationship. Consumer evaluations on a company's websites or other social media channels play a key role in selecting an optimal service provider. Based on those consumer experiences, feedback and reviews, the chapter discusses the Aspect-Based Sentiment Classification by extracting aspects from the consumer feedback using deep learning approaches. The chapter considered RNN, LSTM and GRU algorithms and prioritised different cloud service providers based on the identified aspects of trust, security and cost. The analysis also identifies the RNN model as the best and most efficient regarding its performance, accuracy rates and processing time.

Chapter 5, "Interval Type-2 Fuzzy Decision Analysis Framework based on Online Textual Reviews", discusses that the popularity of the Internet and the development of social media and the volume of online textual reviews (OTRs) has sharply increased. Even though these reviews offer a valuable source of knowledge to address complex decision situations, properly modelling the information in the OTRs is still an open problem. In this chapter, a multi-criteria decision analysis framework for OTRs based on interval type-2 fuzzy sets is developed. First, the OTRs are processed by data cleaning and transformed into interval type-2 fuzzy distributed structures using sentiment analysis. Then, an interval type-2 fuzzy entropy weight model is applied to determine the criteria weights, and subsequently, the Evidential Reasoning (ER) algorithm is used to fuse the interval type-2 fuzzy distributed information and generate the interval-valued expected utility of each alternative. Afterwards, a minimax regret approach is established to rank the obtained interval-valued expected utilities. Finally, a case study is given to illustrate the implementation process of the proposed method.

Chapter 6, "Robust Comprehensive Minimum Cost Consensus Model for Multi-Criteria Group Decision Making: Application in IoT Platform Selection", presents a comprehensive minimum cost consensus (CMCC) model for group decision-making (GDM) problems that provide a new perspective on cost control in consensus-reaching processes (CRPs). Existing models are unsuitable for multi-criteria group decision-making (MCGDM) problems because they neglect the agreement on the final decision that is made according to the importance of the criteria. Therefore, this chapter aims to propose new CMCC models for MCGDM problems, in which an additional constraint is considered to guarantee the agreement on evaluating the alternatives under the criteria. In addition, in real-world decision-making problems, the unit adjustment cost of experts often presents uncertainty. Considering that the disturbance of uncertain data may reduce the quality of the optimal solution, this chapter uses the robust optimisation (RO) method to establish an R-MC-CMCC model to provide uncertainty-stable solutions. Afterwards, the implementation of the proposed framework is shown in an illustrative example related to selecting an Internet of Things (IoT) platform. Finally, a sensitivity analysis regarding the involved parameters is provided.

Acknowledgements

We want to express our sincere gratitude to all those individuals and parties who helped us produce this book. First, we would like to thank all our co-authors and authors who have contributed their expertise, insight and research work to make this book a comprehensive and insightful resource for readers. Thanks to CRC Press/ Taylor & Francis Group for believing in our project and allowing us to publish this book. We thank the reviewers who provided thoughtful feedback and constructive criticism, which helped improve and refine this book's content.

About the Editors

Walayat Hussain is currently the National Head of the Information Technology Discipline at Peter Faber Business School, Australian Catholic University, Australia. He has an academic and industry experience of more than 18 years. Before joining the ACU, he was a lecturer at Victoria University Melbourne, Australia, and a lecturer and post-doctoral research fellow at the University of Technology Sydney, Australia for seven years. He worked as an assistant professor and postgraduate program coordinator in the Department of Computer Science at BUITEMS University for many years. He holds a PhD, master's, postgraduate diploma and bachelor's (Hons.) degrees in Computing and Information Systems. Walayat's research areas are service computing, business intelligence, AI, information systems, computational intelligence, machine learning and decision support systems. He has contributed to theory and application and developed a new approach for making an optimal informed decision in complex systems. He has published over 76 high-quality research documents in the top-ranked ERA-A*, A and JCR/SJR Q1 journals. He is currently an associate editor of *IET – Communications and Forecasting*, an international journal, and has been a guest editor for more than 25 international journals. He has served as the general chair and led the EAI-IoTaaS 2021 7th EAI International Conference on IoT as a Service (December 2021) in Sydney, Australia, co-general chair at BiGIoT-EDU2023 (August 2023) in China, co-general chair at the 3rd International Conference on MMCITARE (March 2022) in India and Sydney and as technical program committee chair at BIG-IoT-EDU (July 2022) in China. He has been a track chair at the 14th IEEE ICEBE in China and a PC member of NBiS in 2016 in the Czech Republic. Currently, he serves as a member of the Peter Faber Business School Executive Committee and the Faculty Learning and Teaching Academy member. He also served as a member of the VUBS HDR Committee at Victoria University and as a member of the Board of Faculty and Studies at BUITEMS University for three years. He is a fellow of the European Alliance for Invocation (EAI). He is the recipient of the prestigious National Research Award from the Government of Oman in 2021, the VUBS Award for Excellence in Research in 2022, the Best Paper Award at IoTaaS in Australia in 2021, the Best Paper Awards at 3PGCIC in 2015, in 2016 in Poland and South Korea, and the FEIT HDR Publication Award by the UTS, Australia, in 2016.

Honghao Gao is currently with the School of Computer Engineering and Science, Shanghai University, China. He is also a professor at the College of Future Industry, Gachon University, Korea. His research interests include software security with formal methods, cloud/Edge computing and intelligent data processing. He has publications in IEEE TII, IEEE T-ITS, IEEE TNNLS, IEEE TMM, IEEE TSC, IEEE TCC, IEEE TFS, IEEE TNSE, IEEE TNSM, IEEE TCCN, IEEE TGCN, IEEE TCSS, IEEE TETCI, IEEE/ACM TCBB, etc. He was the 2022 recipient of Highly Cited Chinese Researchers by Elsevier and the 2021 recipient of IEEE Outstanding Paper Award for the IEEE Transactions on Industrial Informatics. Prof. Gao is a fellow of the Institution of Engineering and Technology (IET), a fellow of the

British Computer Society (BCS), and a member of the European Academy of Sciences and Arts (EASA). He is the Editor-in-Chief of the *International Journal of Web Information Systems* (IJWIS) and editor of *Wireless Network* (WINE), *The Computer Journal* (COMPJ) and *IET Wireless Sensor Systems* (IET WSS), and associate editor of *IEEE Transactions on Intelligent Transportation Systems* (IEEE T-ITS), *IET Intelligent Transport Systems* (IET ITS), *IET Software, International Journal of Communication Systems* (IJCS), *Journal of Internet Technology* (JIT) and *Engineering Reports* (EngReports). Moreover, he has a broad working experience in a cooperative industry–university research. He is a European Union Institutions-appointed external expert for reviewing and monitoring the EU Project, is a member of the EPSRC Peer Review Associate College for UK Research and Innovation in the UK and a founding member of the IEEE Computer Society Smart Manufacturing Standards Committee.

Fethi Rabhi is a professor at the School of Computer Science and Engineering at the University of New South Wales, Australia. His main research areas are in service-oriented software engineering with a strong focus on business and financial applications. He completed his PhD in Computer Science at the University of Sheffield in 1990 and held several academic appointments in the USA and the UK before joining UNSW in 2000. He is currently actively involved in several research projects in the area of large-scale news and financial market data analysis.

Luis Martínez (Highly Cited Researcher in the World by Clarivate Analytics) is a full Professor of the Computer Science Department at the University of Jaén. His research interests are computational intelligence, machine, fuzzy decision making, computing with words, fuzzy systems, intelligent decision support and recommender systems. He has published more than 250 journals indexed by the SCI, three books, more than 35 book chapters, and more than 200 contributions to International Conferences related to his areas. He co-edited 21 journal special issues on fuzzy preference modelling, soft computing, linguistic decision making, machine learning and fuzzy sets theory. He has been the main researcher in 18 R&D projects. He is a member of the European Society for Fuzzy Logic and Technology and he is an IEEE senior member, Editor in Chief of the *International Journal of Computational Intelligence Systems* and associate editor of the journals *IEEE Transactions on Fuzzy Systems, Knowledge-Based Systems, Information Fusion, Information Sciences, Expert Systems with Applications, Human-centric Computing and Information Sciences*, etc. He received the IFSA Fellow 2021, the Chutian Scholarship from Wuhan University of Technology (2016) and the IEEE Transactions on Fuzzy Systems Outstanding Paper Award twice in 2008 and 2012 (bestowed in 2011 and 2015, respectively). He is a visiting professor at the University of Technology Sydney, the University of Portsmouth (Isambard Kingdom Brunel Fellowship Scheme) and the Wuhan University of Technology (Chutian Scholar), a guest professor at the Southwest Jiaotong University and an honourable professor at Xihua University both in Chengdu. Eventually, he was executive secretary of the Eureka International Board of the Eurekas community from 2017 to 2021 EUSFLAT board member.

List of Contributors

Bapi Dutta
Department of Computer Sciences
Universidad de Jaén
Jaén, Spain

Diego García-Zamora
Department of Computer Sciences
Universidad de Jaén
Jaén, Spain

Yefan Han
Business School
Shanghai University
Shanghai, China
and
Department of Computer Sciences
Universidad de Jaén
Jaén, Spain

Wen He
Department of Computer Sciences
Universidad de Jaén
Jaén, Spain

Shi-Fan He
Decision Sciences Institute
Fuzhou University
Fuzhou, China
and
Department of Computer Sciences
Universidad de Jaén
Jaén, Spain

José Hélio de Brum Müller
Private consultant
Sydney, Australia

Alan Hsiao
Cognitivo, Australia

Walayat Hussain
Peter Faber Business School
Australian Catholic University
Fitzroy, Australia

Álvaro Labella
Department of Computer Sciences
Universidad de Jaén
Jaén, Spain

Wei Liang
Department of Computer Sciences
Universidad de Jaén
Jaén, Spain
and
Decision Science Institute, School of
  Economics & Management
Fuzhou University
Fuzhou, China

Eric Lim
School of Information Systems,
  Technology and Management
UNSW
Sydney, Australia

Luis Martínez
Department of Computer Sciences
Universidad de Jaén
Jaén, Spain

Zoran Milosevic
Deontik, Australia and Institute for
  Integrated and Intelligent Systems
Griffith University
Nathan, Australia

Alan Ng
School of Computer Science and
  Engineering
UNSW
Sydney, Australia

Xiao-Hong Pan
Decision Sciences Institute
Fuzhou University
Fuzhou, China
and
Department of Computer Sciences
Universidad de Jaén
Jaén, Spain

Fethi Rabhi
School of Computer Science and
  Engineering
UNSW
Sydney, Australia

Muhammad Raheel Raza
Firat University
Elazığ, Turkey

Mehdi Rajaeian
Peter Faber Business School
Australian Catholic University
Sydney, Australia

Rosa M. Rodríguez
Department of Computer Sciences
Universidad de Jaén
Jaén, Spain

Felix Tan
School of Information Systems,
  Technology and Management
UNSW
Sydney, Australia

Mingqin Yu
School of Computer Science and
  Engineering
UNSW
Sydney, Australia

1 Application of Choquet–OWA Aggregation Operator to Fuse ELICIT Information

Wen He
Universidad de Jaén, Jaén, Spain

Wei Liang
Universidad de Jaén, Jaén, Spain
Fuzhou University, Fuzhou, China

Álvaro Labella and Rosa M. Rodríguez
Universidad de Jaén, Jaén, Spain

1.1 INTRODUCTION

Real-world decision-making problems are always constrained by human activity, resources, technology, and other conditions that make the decision environment become increasingly complex. Under this context, the experts select one or several alternatives as solutions to the decision problem, which often need to be evaluated over a number of relevant criteria. Such problems are common in various fields, such as supplier selection (Kabadayi & Dehghanimohammadabadi, 2022; Ulutaş et al., 2021), emergency decision making (Liang & Wang, 2020), evaluation of renewable energy (Almutairi et al., 2022), etc., and they are known as multi-criteria decision-making (MCDM) (Cables, Lamata, & Verdegay, 2016; Keeny & Raiffa, 1976) problems.

Due to the complexity of the decision environment and the ambiguity of the information, it is difficult for experts to give their preferences precisely, preferring to express their opinions in terms of linguistic information rather than numerical values, which is more in line with their way of thinking. For this reason, Zadeh introduced the fuzzy linguistic approach (FLA) and the concept of linguistic variable (Zadeh, 1975a, 1975b, 1975c) to model the uncertainty inherent in linguistic information. In consequence, the use of linguistic information for modeling experts' preferences inevitably implies to perform computations with linguistic information. The Computing with Words (CW) methodology allows carrying out linguistic computations following a clear premise, the results have to be represented linguistically and derived from linguistic inputs, simulating the human beings' reasoning process.

DOI: 10.1201/9781003340621-1

1

Since the emergence of FLA, many FLA-based computational models have been proposed, such as the 2-tuple linguistic model (Herrera & Martínez, 2000a), the comparative linguistic expressions (CLEs) (Rodríguez, Martínez, & Herrera, 2013), or the hesitant fuzzy linguistic term sets (HFLTSs) (Rodríguez, Martínez, & Herrera, 2012), and their extensions (Tang & Zheng, 2006; Wang & Hao, 2006; Wang, Yang, & Xu, 2006a). However, the majority of them have certain limitations (Rodríguez, Labella, & Martíncz, 2016). For example, the 2-tuple linguistic model follows a CW approach, but it does not allow modeling experts' hesitancy. On the other hand, CLEs and HFLTSs allow a flexible and rich representation of experts' hesitancy, but the interpretability of results in existing computational models and the loss of information in the CW (Zadeh, 1975a, 1975b, 1975c) process may limit their use. To deal with these drawbacks, Labella et al. (2019) proposed a linguistic representation model based on extended CLEs (Rodríguez et al., 2013) with symbolic translation (ELICIT). The ELICIT computational model follows a CW scheme which models experts' hesitation and obtains more precise and interpretable results than the previous proposals. These remarkable characteristics have led to several fruitful contributions in the literature (Dutta et al., 2019; He et al., 2021a; He et al., 2021b; He et al., 2022; Labella et al., 2020).

In the same way that representing information is key in the decision process, the aggregation of such information plays also a pivotal role in the decision-making process by combining individual pieces of information into a collective value. The aggregation operators have a significant impact on the decision process, since an inappropriate selection of them may lead to irrational results. One of the most widely used aggregation operators is the ordered weighted aggregation (OWA) operator (Yager, 1988), whose weights are position-dependent. However, the OWA weights are generally obtained by linguistic quantifiers (Yager, 1996) under the assumption of complete independence between criteria, which may be unrealistic in several MCDM problems. In other words, the criteria weights used by the aggregation operator should be generated keeping in mind the different interrelationships between the criteria for each alternative. In this sense, other tools are able to capture the relationships between criteria (Ali, Mahmood, & Yang, 2020; Chen, Chin, & Tsui, 2019; Dutta et al., 2019). Among them, the Choquet integral (Chen et al., 2020; Choquet, 1954; Meng, Chen, & Tang, 2021) is able to identify complex interactions between criteria by means of the definition of a predefined fuzzy measure.

Therefore, considering the advantages of the ELICIT information in terms of precision and interpretability of the decision results and the need for proposing aggregation operators able not only to fuse the ELICIT information but also to capture the relations between the criteria, here we propose an OWA operator for ELICIT information, called ELICIT-Choquet-OWA operator. The aggregation operator first requires transforming the ELICIT information into trapezoidal fuzzy numbers (TrFNs), which are convex and normal fuzzy numbers with a certain research base (Abbasbandy & Hajjari, 2009; Dombi & Jónás, 2020; Kumar et al., 2010; Savitha & Mary, 2017; Yager, 2008), and then calculates the OWA weights by the Choquet integral to consider the interrelationships between the criteria in the aggregation process. On this basis, a new MCDM model is further proposed. Thus, the novelties of this chapter are the following ones:

1. Definition of the ELICIT-Choquet-OWA operator to aggregate ELICIT information considering the interrelationships between criteria by means of the Choquet integral and the OWA operator.
2. A brief study of the properties of the ELICIT-Choquet-OWA operator is introduced.
3. A novel approach for MCDM problems on the basis of the proposed aggregation operator is developed.

The rest of this chapter is organized as follows. Section 1.2 reviews some related concepts, such as the 2-tuple linguistic computation model, ELICIT information, fuzzy measure, Choquet integral, and the OWA operator. Section 1.3 proposes the ELICIT-Choquet-OWA operator. Moreover, a brief study of the properties of the ELICIT-Choquet-OWA operator is presented in Section 1.4. Section 1.5 introduces a new MCDM model based on the proposed operator, and a case study is applied to show its feasibility and applicability in Section 1.6. Finally, some conclusions are pointed out in Section 1.7.

1.2   PRELIMINARIES

In this section, we review some basic concepts of the 2-tuple linguistic model, ELICIT information, the Choquet integral, and the OWA operator that are relevant to the construction of our new aggregation operator.

1.2.1   2-TUPLE LINGUISTIC MODEL

Herrera and Martínez (2000b) introduced the concept of 2-tuple linguistic information to overcome the shortcomings related to the lack of accuracy and interpretability of classical models. This model treats the linguistic domain as continuous and performs computation without approximation.

For notational purpose, let $S = \{s_0, s_1, s_2, \cdots, s_g\}$ be a linguistic term set of odd $g + 1$ granularity whose semantics satisfies the following properties:

1. The set has an inherent natural order, shown as $s_i \leq s_j$ if and only if $i \leq j$.
2. The negative operator $\text{Neg}(\cdot)$ is defined on this set as $s_i = \text{Neg}(s_{g-i})$.

The 2-tuple linguistic information is represented by a tuple $(s_i, \alpha) \in \bar{S} := S \times [-0.5, 0.5]$, where s_i refers to a linguistic term belonging to S and α, so-called symbolic translation, is a numerical value that represents the displacement of the s_i fuzzy membership function:

$$\alpha \in \begin{cases} [-0.5, 0.5) & \text{if } s_i \in \{s_1, s_2, \ldots, s_{g-1}\} \\ [0, 0.5) & \text{if } s_i = s_0 \\ [-0.5, 0] & \text{if } s_i = s_g \end{cases} \tag{1.1}$$

The 2-tuple linguistic value can be translated into a numerical value $x \in [0, g]$ as follows:

Proposition 1

(Herrera & Martínez, 2000b) Let $S = \{s_0, \ldots s_g\}$ be a linguistic term set. Then, the function $\Delta_S^{-1} : \bar{S} \rightarrow [0, g]$ is defined by

$$\Delta_S^{-1}(\bar{s}_i) = i + \alpha = x \qquad (1.2)$$

is a bijection whose inverse $\Delta_S : [0, g] \rightarrow \bar{S}$ is given by

$$\Delta_S(x) = \left(s_{\text{round}(x)}, x - \text{round}(x)\right), \forall x \in [0, g], \qquad (1.3)$$

where round(·) *is the function that assigns the closest integer number $i \in \{0, \ldots, g\}$.*

Remark 1 Noted that the 2-tuple linguistic value $(s_i, 0) \in \bar{S}$ can be used to represent the single linguistic term s_i.

1.2.2   ELICIT INFORMATION

ELICIT information (Labella et al., 2019) is a new linguistic representation model to depict experts' hesitancy and attain more precise and interpretable results than previous proposals. The ELICIT information is based on CLEs and, as they do, it is generated from a context-free grammar. Whilethe CLEs are built by using single linguistic terms (Rodríguez et al., 2013), the ELICIT expressions replace them by 2-tuple linguistic values as follows Labella et al. (2019):

Definition 1

Let G_H be a context-free grammar and $S = \{s_0, \ldots s_g\}$ be a linguistic term set, then- the elements of $G_H = (V_N, V_T, I, P)$ are given by:

$$V_N = \big\{(\text{continuous primary term}), (\text{composite term}), (\text{unary relation}),$$

$$(\text{binary relation}), (\text{conjunction})\big\}$$

$$V_T = \Big\{\text{at least, at most, between, and}, (s_0, \alpha)^{\gamma}, (s_1, \alpha)^{\gamma}, \ldots, (s_g, \alpha)^{\gamma}\Big\}$$

$$I \in V_N$$

The production rules P defined in an extended Backus–Naur Form are as follows:

$P = \{I ::= (\text{continuous primary term}) \mid (\text{composite term})$

$(\text{composite term}) ::= (\text{unary relation})(\text{continuous primary term}) \mid$

$(\text{binary relation})(\text{continuous primary term})(\text{conjunction})$

$(\text{continuous primary term})$

$(\text{continuous primary term}) ::= (s_0, \alpha)^\gamma \mid (s_1, \alpha)^\gamma \mid ... \mid (s_g, \alpha)^\gamma$

$(\text{unary relation}) ::= \text{at least} \mid \text{at most}$

$(\text{binary relation}) ::= \text{between}$

$(\text{conjunction}) ::= \text{and}\}$

According to the previous grammar, four different ELICIT expressions can be obtained: (1) $(s_i, \alpha)^\gamma$, (2) "at least $(s_i, \alpha)^\gamma$", (3) "at most $(s_i, \alpha)^\gamma$", and (4) "between $(s_i, \alpha_1)^{\gamma_1}$ and $(s_j, \alpha_2)^{\gamma_2}$". For the sake of clarity, these expressions are denoted here by an expression $\left[\overline{s}_i, \overline{s}_j\right]_{\gamma_1, \gamma_2}$ (García-Zamora et al., 2022), where $\overline{s}_i, \overline{s}_j \in \overline{S}, i \leq j$ are two 2-tuple linguistic values. Notice the ELICIT values consider two parameters γ_1, γ_2 which guarantee that no information is lost during the computations with these expressions. In addition, it should be noted that any TrFN (Zadeh, 1965) can be unequivocally represented as an ELICIT value, as discussed below.

Remark 2 A TrFN is a function $T \equiv T(a, b, c, d) : [0, 1] \to [0, 1]$ of the form

$$T(x) = \begin{cases} 0 & \text{if } 0 \leq x \leq a \\ \dfrac{x-a}{b-a} & \text{if } a < x < b \\ 1 & \text{if } b \leq x \leq c \quad \forall x \in [0,1] \\ \dfrac{d-x}{d-c} & \text{if } c < x < d \\ 0 & \text{if } d \leq x \leq 1 \end{cases} \tag{1.4}$$

for certain $0 \leq a \leq b \leq c \leq d \leq 1$. For the sake of clarity, the set of all TrFNs on the interval [0, 1] will be denoted by

$$\{T\} = \{T : [0,1] \to [0,1] : T \text{ is a TrFN}\}.$$

The ELICIT representation model was proposed together with a CW-based computational model in which linguistic results are obtained from linguistic inputs. This scheme is shown in Figure 1.1 and can be described by the following three processes:

1. **Translation process:** The ELICIT expressions are transformed into equivalent TrFNs by computing their fuzzy envelope function ζ^{-1}, which is defined as follows García-Zamora et al. (2022):

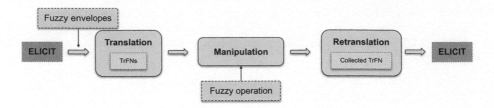

FIGURE 1.1   The ELICIT-CW scheme.

Definition 2

Let $\bar{\bar{S}}$ be the set of all possible ELICIT values. Then the mapping ζ^{-1} is given by:

$$\zeta^{-1} : \bar{\bar{S}} \to \mathcal{T}$$
$$\left[\bar{s}_1, \bar{s}_2\right]_{\gamma_1, \gamma_2} \mapsto T(a, b, c, d) \tag{1.5}$$

and allows computing the fuzzy representation of an ELICIT expression as follows:

$$a = \gamma_1 + \max\left\{\frac{\Delta_S^{-1}(\bar{s}_1) - \dfrac{1}{g}}{g}, 0\right\}, \quad b = \frac{\Delta_S^{-1}(\bar{s}_1)}{g},$$

$$d = \gamma_2 + \min\left\{\frac{\Delta_S^{-1}(\bar{s}_2) + \dfrac{1}{g}}{g}, 1\right\}, \quad c = \frac{\Delta_S^{-1}(\bar{s}_2)}{g}. \tag{1.6}$$

2. **Manipulation process:** The TrFNs are manipulated by aggregation operators based on fuzzy arithmetic operations to obtain a collective TrFN, denoted as $\tilde{\beta}$.
3. **Retranslation process:** The TrFN $\tilde{\beta}$ is retranslated into its equivalent ELICIT expression, by using the function ζ defined as follows García-Zamora et al. (2022):

Definition 3

Let $\bar{\bar{S}}$ be the set of all possible ELICIT values. Then the mapping ζ given by:

$$\zeta : \mathcal{T} \to \bar{\bar{S}}$$
$$T(a, b, c, d) \mapsto \left[\bar{s}_1, \bar{s}_2\right]_{\gamma_1, \gamma_2} \tag{1.7}$$

where

$$\bar{s}_1 = \Delta_S(gb) \quad \gamma_1 = a - \max\left\{b - \frac{1}{g^2}, 0\right\}$$

$$\bar{s}_2 = \Delta_S(gc) \quad \gamma_2 = d - \min\left\{c + \frac{1}{g^2}, 1\right\}$$

(1.8)

1.2.3 CHOQUET INTEGRAL

In MCDM problems, the Choquet integral (Choquet, 1954) based on a fuzzy measure is a widely and successfully used tool for modeling complex interactions between the criteria and capturing the uncertainty inherent in the measurement of such relationships. To clarify the definition of the Choquet integral used in this chapter, we will first review Sugeno's fuzzy measure (Murofushi and Sugeno, 1989; Sugeno, 1993) and then perform the Choquet integral.

Definition 4

Assume that X is a set and $\mathcal{P}(X)$ is the power set of X which is an σ- algebra. A fuzzy measure defined on X is a mapping $\mu : \mathcal{P}(X) \to [0,1]$, such that

(1) $\mu(\varnothing) = 0$ and $\mu(X) = 1$.
(2)   If $A \subset B, \forall A, B \subset X$, then $\mu(A) \leq \mu(B)$.
(3) $\mu(A \cup B) = \mu(A) + \mu(B) + \lambda\mu(A)\mu(B), \forall A, B \subset X$ and $A \cap B = \varnothing, \lambda \geq -1$.

(4)   If $A_n \subset X, \forall n \in \mathbf{N}$ and $A_n \subset A_{n+1}$, then $\mu\left(\bigcup_{n=1}^{\infty} A_n\right) = \lim_{n \to \infty} \mu(A_n)$.

(5)   If $A_n \subset X, \forall n \in \mathbf{N}$ and $A_{n+1} \subset A_n$, then $\mu\left(\bigcap_{n=1}^{\infty} A_n\right) = \lim_{n \to \infty} \mu(A_n)$.

Subsequently, the definitions of the Choquet integral will be presented based on the predefined fuzzy measure.

Definition 5

Grabisch & Roubens (2000) Let $X = \{x_1, x_2, \ldots, x_n\}$ be a nonempty set and μ be the fuzzy measure on X. The discrete Choquet integral of a function $f: X \to \mathbf{R}^+$ with respect to μ is defined as

$$(C)\int f d\mu \triangleq \sum_{i=1}^{n} f\left(x_{\sigma(i)}\right)\left[\mu\left(A_{\sigma(i)}\right) - \mu\left(A_{\sigma(i-1)}\right)\right]$$

(1.9)

where $\sigma : \{1, \ldots, n\} \to \{1, \ldots, n\}$ is a permutation function such that $f(x_{\sigma(i-1)}) \geq f(x_{\sigma(i)})$ for all $i = 1, \ldots, n$. $A_{\sigma(k)} \triangleq \{x_{\sigma(1)}, \ldots, x_{\sigma(k)}\}, k \geq 1$, and $\mu(A_{\sigma(0)}) = 0, \mu(A_{\sigma(n)}) = 1$.

1.2.4   OWA OPERATOR

A spectrum of studies have been carried out in the field of aggregation operators. One of the widely used is the OWA aggregation operator (Merigó & Casanovas, 2008; Yager, 1988, 2008; Zarghami, Szidarovszky, & Ardakanian, 2008; Hussain, Merigó, & Raza, 2022c; Hussain et al., 2022b; Hussain et al., 2022a).

Definition 6

Yager (1988) Let $\mathbf{R}$ be the set of all real numbers. An OWA operator is defined as a mapping $\Phi_{OWA} : \mathbf{R}^n \to \mathbf{R}$, which is associated with a weighting vector $(\omega_1, ..., \omega_n)$ verifying the properties $\omega_i \in [0, 1]$ and $\sum_{i=1}^{n} \omega_i = 1$, such that

$$\Phi_{OWA}\left(a_1, a_2, ..., a_n\right) = \sum_{k=1}^{n} \omega_k a_{\sigma(k)} \tag{1.10}$$

where $\sigma : \{1, ..., n\} \to \{1, ..., n\}$ is a permutation function such that $a_{\sigma(k)}$ is the kth largest element of the n-dimensional vector $(a_1, ..., a_n)$.

Several extensions of the OWA operator have been proposed to deal with TrFNs in the literature (Garg, Maiti, & Kumar, 2022; Fei et al., 2019; Wang & Deng, 2019). In this contribution, we focus on the OWA operator to fuse ELICIT information because of its relation with our proposal. The ELICIT-OWA operator replaces the set of all real numbers $\mathbf{R}$ by the set of all possible ELICIT expressions, denoted as $\bar{S}$, which are transformed into TrFNs to perform the computations (He et al., 2021c).

Definition 7

Let $\bar{S}$ be a set of all possible ELICIT expressions. The ELICIT-OWA operator is defined as a mapping $\Phi_{ELICIT\text{-}OWA} : \bar{S}^n \to \bar{S}$, which is associated with a weighting vector $(\omega_1, ..., \omega_n)$ verifying the properties $\omega_i \in [0, 1]$ and $\sum_{i=1}^{n} \omega_i = 1$, such that

$$\Phi_{ELICIT\text{-}OWA}\left(x_1, x_2, ..., x_n\right) = \zeta\left(\sum_{k=1}^{n} \omega_k \zeta^{-1}\left(x_{\sigma(k)}\right)\right) \tag{1.11}$$

where $\sigma : \{1, ..., n\} \to \{1, ..., n\}$ is a permutation function such that $x_{\sigma(k)}$ is the kth largest element of the n-dimensional vector $(x_1, ..., x_n)$.

1.3 A NEW AGGREGATION OPERATOR FOR ELICIT INFORMATION

This section introduces a new OWA operator to fuse ELICIT information and whose weights are generated by using the fuzzy measure of Choquet integral in order to take into account the interrelationship between criteria in the aggregation process.

Definition 8

Let $\bar{S}$ be a set of all possible ELICIT expressions, $\{C_i\}_{i=1}^n$ be a nonempty set of criteria, and μ be a predefined fuzzy measure on $\{C_i\}_{i=1}^n$. The ELICIT-Choquet-OWA operator is defined as a mapping $\Phi_{\text{ELICIT-Choquet-OWA}} : \bar{S}^n \rightarrow \bar{S}$ such that:

$$\Phi_{\text{ELICIT-Choquet-OWA}}\left(x_1,\ldots,x_n\right) \triangleq \zeta\left(\bigoplus_{n}^{i=1} \zeta^{-1}\left(x_{\sigma(i)}\right)\omega_i \right)$$

$$= \zeta\left(\sum_{i=1}^n a_i\omega_i, \sum_{i=1}^n b_i\omega_i, \sum_{i=1}^n c_i\omega_i, \sum_{i=1}^n d_i\omega_i \right) \tag{1.12}$$

$$\text{with}\quad \omega_i \triangleq \psi\left(\mu\left(A_{\sigma(i)}\right)\right) - \psi\left(\mu\left(A_{\sigma(i-1)}\right)\right)$$

where $\oplus$ is the general addition between TrFN. $\sigma(\cdot)$ is a permutation function of $\{1, \ldots, n\}$, such that $x_{\sigma(i-1)} \geqslant x_{\sigma(i)}$ for all $i = 1, \ldots, n$. The mapping $\psi(\cdot) : [0, 1] \rightarrow [0, 1]$ is used to compute the weights $A_{\sigma(i)} \triangleq \{C_{\sigma(1)}, \ldots, C_{\sigma(i)}\}$ and $\mu(A_{\sigma(0)}) = 0$, $\mu(A_{\sigma(n)}) = 1$. $C_{\sigma(i)}$ is the criterion corresponding to $x_{\sigma(i)}$. $\zeta^{-1}(x_{\sigma(i)}) = T(a_i, b_i, c_i, d_i)$ is the equivalent TrFN corresponding to the ELICIT expression $x_{\sigma(i)} \in \bar{S}$ for all $i = 1, \ldots, n$, and ζ is the inverse function of ζ^{-1}.

Remark 3 If $\psi(x) = x$, that is, $\omega_i = \mu(A_{\sigma(i)}) - \mu(A_{\sigma(i-1)})$, and if $\mu(A_{\sigma(i)})$ is a crisp number for all i $1, \ldots, n$, then it is obvious that $\omega_i \geq 0$ and $\sum_{i=0}^n \omega_i = 1$. Hence, the ELICIT-Choquet-OWA operator can be regarded as the classical Choquet integral applied to ELICIT information.

1.4 PROPERTIES OF THE ELICIT-CHOQUET-OWA OPERATOR

This section briefly examines some properties of the ELICIT-Choquet-OWA operator such as idempotency, commutativity, monotonicity, and boundedness.

Theorem 2

(Idempotency) Let Φ be an ELICIT-Choquet-OWA operator. If $x_i = x$ for all $i = 1, 2, \ldots, n$, then

$$\Phi\left(x_1, x_2, \ldots, x_n\right) = x. \tag{1.13}$$

Proof. Since $x_i = x$, that is, $\zeta^{-1}(x_{\sigma(i)}) = \zeta^{-1}(x)$ for all $i = 1, 2, \ldots, n$, then

$$\Phi\left(x_1, x_2, \ldots, x_n\right) = \zeta\left(\overset{i=1}{\underset{n}{\oplus}} \zeta^{-1}\left(x_{\sigma(i)}\right)\omega_i\right)$$

$$= \zeta\left(\overset{i=1}{\underset{n}{\oplus}} \zeta^{-1}\left(x\right)\omega_i\right)$$

$$= \zeta\left(\zeta^{-1}\left(x\right)\right)\left(\sum_{i=1}^{n}\omega_i\right)$$

Since $\displaystyle\sum_{i=1}^{n}\omega_i = 1$ and $\zeta(\zeta^{-1}(x)) = x$, then

$$\Phi\left(x_1, x_2, \ldots, x_n\right) = \zeta\left(\zeta^{-1}\left(x\right)\right)\left(\sum_{i=1}^{n}\omega_i\right) = x \tag{1.14}$$

Therefore,

$$\Phi\left(x_1, x_2, \ldots, x_n\right) = x. \tag{1.15}$$

Theorem 3

(Commutativity) Let Φ be an ELICIT-Choquet-OWA operator. Then

$$\Phi\left(x'_1, x'_2, \ldots, x'_n\right) = \Phi\left(x_1, x_2, \ldots, x_n\right) \tag{1.16}$$

where $(x'_1, x'_2, \ldots, x'_n)$ is any permutation of elements in $(x_1, x_2, \ldots, x_n)$.

Proof. Let $\sigma: \{1, \ldots, n\} \to \{1, \ldots, n\}$ be a permutation function applied to $(x_1, x_2, \ldots, x_n)$ such that $x_{\sigma(1)} > x_{\sigma(2)} > \ldots > x_{\sigma(n)}$, thus

$$\Phi\left(x_1, x_2, \ldots, x_n\right) = \Phi\left(x_{\sigma(1)}, x_{\sigma(2)}, \ldots, x_{\sigma(n)}\right). \tag{1.17}$$

Similarly, apply σ to $(x'_1, x'_2, \ldots, x'_n)$ to obtain $x'_{\sigma(1)} > x'_{\sigma(2)} > \ldots > x'_{\sigma(n)}$, then

$$\left(x'_{\sigma(1)}, x'_{\sigma(2)}, \ldots, x'_{\sigma(n)}\right) = \left(x_{\sigma(1)}, x_{\sigma(2)}, \ldots, x_{\sigma(n)}\right) \tag{1.18}$$

and

$$\Phi\left(x'_1, x'_2, \ldots, x'_n\right) = \Phi\left(x'_{\sigma(1)}, x'_{\sigma(2)}, \ldots, x'_{\sigma(n)}\right) = \Phi\left(x_{\sigma(1)}, x_{\sigma(2)}, \ldots, x_{\sigma(n)}\right) \quad (1.19)$$

Therefore,

$$\Phi\left(x'_1, x'_2, \ldots, x'_n\right) = \Phi\left(x_1, x_2, \ldots, x_n\right). \quad (1.20)$$

Theorem 4

(Monotonicity) Let Φ be an ELICIT-Choquet-OWA operator, and $(x_1, x_2, \ldots, x_n)$ and $(z_1, z_2, \ldots, z_n)$ be two n-dimensional vectors of ELICIT expressions such that $x_i \geq z_i$ for all $i = 1, 2, \ldots, n$, that is, their corresponding fuzzy numbers $\zeta^{-1}(x_i)$ and $\zeta^{-1}(z_i)$ also satisfy $\zeta^{-1}(x_i) \geq \zeta^{-1}(z_i)$. Then

$$\Phi\left(x_1, x_2, \ldots, x_n\right) \geq \Phi\left(z_1, z_2, \ldots, z_n\right) \quad (1.21)$$

Proof. According to Definition 8,

$$\Phi\left(x_1, x_2, \ldots, x_n\right) = \zeta\left(\overset{i=1}{\underset{n}{\oplus}} \zeta^{-1}\left(x_{\sigma(i)}\right) \omega_i\right) \quad (1.22)$$

and

$$\Phi\left(z_1, z_2, \ldots, z_n\right) = \zeta\left(\overset{i=1}{\underset{n}{\oplus}} \zeta^{-1}\left(z_{\sigma(i)}\right) \omega_i\right). \quad (1.23)$$

Since $x_i \geq z_i$, that is, $\zeta^{-1}(x_i) \geq \zeta^{-1}(z_i)$ for all i, we have

$$\begin{aligned}
\Phi\left(x_1, x_2, \ldots, x_n\right) &= \zeta\left(\overset{i=1}{\underset{n}{\oplus}} \zeta^{-1}\left(x_{\sigma(i)}\right) \omega_i\right) \\
&\geq \zeta\left(\overset{i=1}{\underset{n}{\oplus}} \zeta^{-1}\left(z_{\sigma(i)}\right) \omega_i\right) \\
&= \Phi\left(z_1, z_2, \ldots, z_n\right).
\end{aligned} \quad (1.24)$$

Therefore,

$$\Phi\left(x_1, x_2, \ldots, x_n\right) = \Phi\left(z_1, z_2, \ldots, z_n\right). \quad (1.25)$$

Theorem 5

(Boundedness) Let Φ *be a ELICIT-Choquet-OWA operator. Then,*

$$x^* \geq \Phi(x_1, x_2, \ldots, x_n) \geq x_* \tag{1.26}$$

where $\zeta^{-1}(x_*) \leqslant \zeta^{-1}(x_i) \leqslant \zeta^{-1}(x^*)$ *for all* $i = 1, 2, \ldots, n$.

Proof. Applying Theorems 2 and 4, it is obvious that

$$x^* \geq \Phi(x_1, x_2, \ldots, x_n) \geq x_*. \tag{1.27}$$

1.5   A NOVEL MCDM MODEL

This section proposes a new MCDM model based on an ELICIT-Choquet-OWA operator. Moreover, a case study is presented here to show its feasibility and practicality.

A MCDM problem is constructed by a decision matrix, which involves a set of possible alternatives $\{A_1, \ldots, A_n\}$ and a finite set of criteria $\{C_1, \ldots, C_m\}$ for all $m, n \geq 2$. It is given as follows:

$$
\mathcal{M}_{\overline{S}} =
\begin{bmatrix}
 & C_1 & \cdots & C_i & \cdots & C_j & \cdots & C_m \\
A_1 & m_{11} & \cdots & m_{1i} & \cdots & m_{1j} & \cdots & m_{1m} \\
\vdots & \vdots & \ddots & \vdots & \ddots & \vdots & \ddots & \vdots \\
A_i & m_{i1} & \cdots & m_{ii} & \cdots & m_{ij} & \cdots & m_{im} \\
\vdots & \vdots & \ddots & \vdots & \ddots & \vdots & \ddots & \vdots \\
A_j & m_{j1} & \cdots & m_{ji} & \cdots & m_{jj} & \cdots & m_{jm} \\
\vdots & \vdots & \ddots & \vdots & \ddots & \vdots & \ddots & \vdots \\
A_n & m_{n1} & \cdots & m_{ni} & \cdots & m_{nj} & \cdots & m_{nm}
\end{bmatrix}
$$

In this proposal, the assessment m_{ij} provided by an expert is modeled by ELICIT expressions, $\overline{\overline{S}}$, based on a linguistic term set $S = \{s_0, s_1, s_2, \ldots, s_g\}$ to express his/her opinion to the alternative A_i over the criterion C_j. Keeping in mind the ELICIT-CW scheme represented in Figure 1.1, the solving process of the proposed MCDM model consists of the following three steps as shown in Figure 1.2.

Step 1:   The decision matrix M is constructed by an expert who uses CLEs to express his/her opinions, which are then transformed into $\mathcal{M}_{\overline{S}} = (m_{ij})_{n \times m}$ using ELICIT information.

Step 2:   The ELICIT-CW scheme is used to handle the matrix $\mathcal{M}_{\overline{S}} = (m_{ij})_{n \times m}$.

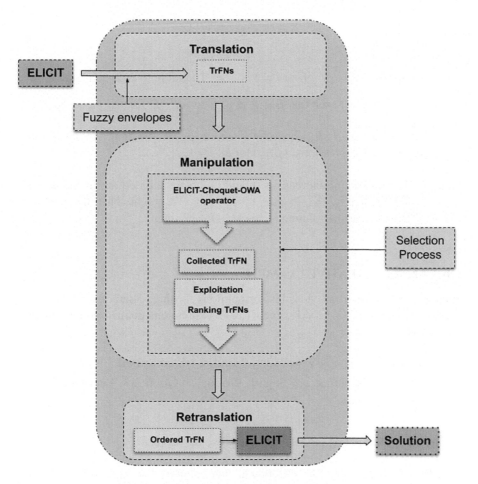

FIGURE 1.2   The ELICIT-CWs scheme for a MCDM problem.

(1) By means of the fuzzy envelope function $\zeta^{-1}(\cdot)$, m_{ij} is equivalently transformed into TrFN as follows:

$$T_j^i = \zeta^{-1}\left(m_{ij}\right). \tag{1.28}$$

(2) During the manipulation, the proposed ELICIT-Choquet-OWA operator is applied to fuse TrFNs, which should first define the weights and then aggregate the TrFNs to obtain a collective TrFN.
   (i)   The weights of the ELICIT-Choquet-OWA operator are calculated according to the predefined fuzzy measure on the criteria.
   (ii) Applying the ELICIT-Choquet-OWA operator to each alternative $\mathcal{A}_i$ yields the vector result $\mathcal{R} = \left\{\tilde{\beta}_i\right\}_{n \times 1}$ with $\tilde{\beta}_i = T^i\left(a_i, b_i, c_i, d_i\right)$ for all $i = 1, \ldots, n$ by the formula

$$\tilde{\beta}_i = \overset{j=1}{\underset{m}{\oplus}} T^i_{\sigma(j)} \omega_j. \tag{1.29}$$

(iii) Rank TrFNs $\tilde{\beta}_i$ for all $i = 1, \ldots, n$. Therefore, σ is a permutation of $\{1, 2, \ldots, n\}$ such that $\tilde{\beta}_{\sigma(1)} \succ \tilde{\beta}_{\sigma(2)} \succ \ldots \succ \tilde{\beta}_{\sigma(n)}$.

(3) The ordered TrFNs $\tilde{\beta}_{\sigma(i)}$ are retranslated using the function ζ to obtain the final ELICIT expression $\zeta\left(\tilde{\beta}_{\sigma(i)}\right)$ for all $i = 1, 2, \ldots, n$.

Step 3:　The ranking of alternatives should be obtained based on the reordered TrFNs, that is, $\mathcal{A}_{\sigma(1)} \succ \mathcal{A}_{\sigma(2)} \succ \ldots \succ \mathcal{A}_{\sigma(n)}$. We might select the alternative $\mathcal{A}_{\sigma(1)}$ as the solution to this MCDM problem.

1.6　AN ILLUSTRATIVE EXAMPLE

Suppose that an expert provides his/her opinions for three alternatives $\{\mathcal{A}_1, \mathcal{A}_2, \mathcal{A}_3\}$ over four criteria $\{C_1, C_2, C_3, C_4\}$ using ELICIT expressions defined on the linguistic nine-terms set

$$S = \{s_0 = \text{None}; s_1 = \text{Very Bad}; s_2 = \text{Bad}; s_3 = \text{Slightly Bad};$$
$$s_4 = \text{Indifference}; s_5 = \text{Slightly Good}; s_6 = \text{Good}; s_7 = \text{Very Good};$$
$$s_8 = \text{Perfect}\}.$$

The proposed MCDM model is used to solve the problem.

Step 1:　The expert uses CLEs to elicit his/her opinions that can be reformulated to ELICIT expressions by adding to each linguistic term $\alpha = 0$ and $\gamma = 0$ as shown below.

$$\mathcal{M} = \begin{bmatrix} & C_1 & C_2 & C_3 & C_4 \\ \mathcal{A}_1 & (s_4,0)^0 & (s_5,0)^0 & \text{between}(s_6,0)^0 \text{ and }(s_7,0)^0 & (s_6,0)^0 \\ \mathcal{A}_2 & \text{at least}(s_7,0)^0 & (s_6,0)^0 & \text{at least}(s_6,0)^0 & (s_5,0)^0 \\ \mathcal{A}_3 & (s_4,0)^0 & (s_7,0)^0 & (s_5,0)^0 & (s_6,0)^0 \end{bmatrix}$$

In sight of this, the matrix M employing $\overline{\overline{S}}$ should be rebuilt as follows:

$$\mathcal{M}_{\overline{\overline{S}}} = \begin{bmatrix} & C_1 & C_2 & C_3 & C_4 \\ \mathcal{A}_1 & (s_4,0)_0 & (s_5,0)_0 & [(s_6,0),(s_7,0)]_{00} & (s_6,0)_0 \\ \mathcal{A}_2 & [(s_7,0),(s_8,0)]_{00} & (s_6,0)_0 & [(s_6,0),(s_8,0)]_{00} & (s_5,0)_0 \\ \mathcal{A}_3 & (s_4,0)_0 & (s_7,0)_0 & (s_5,0)_0 & (s_6,0)_0 \end{bmatrix}$$

Step 2:   The ELICIT-CW scheme is applied to deal with the matrix $\mathcal{M}_{\overline{S}} = \left(m_{ij} \right)_{3 \times 4}$.

(1) The ELICIT expression, m_{ij}, is transformed into TrFN for all $i = 1,2,3$; $j = 1,2,3,4$ (see García-Zamora et al. (2022) for futher detail). For instance:

$$\varsigma^{-1}\left(m_{11} \right) = T_1^1 \left(0.375, 0.5, 0.5, 0.625 \right);$$
$$\varsigma^{-1}\left(m_{13} \right) = T_3^1 \left(0.625, 0.75, 0.875, 1 \right);$$
$$\varsigma^{-1}\left(m_{21} \right) = T_1^2 \left(0.75, 0.875, 1, 1 \right).$$

(2) The ELICIT-Choquet-OWA operator is applied to aggregate TrFNs.

   i. Computing the weights for the ELICIT-Choquet-OWA operator.

      a) It should be pointed out that, for each alternative, the corresponding criteria have different interrelationships and importance. Therefore, the criteria weights cannot be fixed but computed by means of the predefined fuzzy measure over criteria. Assume that the given predefined fuzzy measure on $\{C_1, C_2, C_3, C_4\}$ is presented as follows:

$$\mu(\varnothing) = 0; \; \mu\left(\{C_1\} \right) = 0.2; \; \mu\left(\{C_2\} \right) = 0.4; \; \mu\left(\{C_3\} \right) = 0.3;$$
$$\mu\left(\{C_4\} \right) = 0.37; \; \mu\left(\{C_1, C_2\} \right) = 0.5; \; \mu\left(\{C_1, C_3\} \right) = 0.48;$$
$$\mu\left(\{C_1, C_4\} \right) = 0.65; \; \mu\{C_2, C_3\} = 0.6; \; \mu\{C_2, C_4\} = 0.8;$$
$$\mu\left(\{C_3, C_4\} \right) = 0.7; \; \mu\left(\{C_1, C_2, C_3\} \right) = 0.75;$$
$$\mu\left(\{C_1, C_2, C_4\} \right) = 0.8; \; \mu\left(\{C_2, C_3, C_4\} \right) = 0.95;$$
$$\mu\left(\{C_1, C_3, C_4\} \right) = 0.87; \; \mu\left(\{C_1, C_2, C_3, C_4\} \right) = 1;$$

      b) In this MCDM problem, for each alternative $A_i \left(\forall i = 1, 2, 3 \right)$, using the ranking approach introduced by Wang et al. (2006b), and taking into account the definition of the ELICIT-Choquet-OWA operator, the reordering of $\{m_{i1}, m_{i2}, m_{i3}, m_{i4}\}$ needs to be obtained, which is as follows:

$$m_{13} \succ m_{14} \succ m_{12} \succ m_{11};$$
$$m_{21} \succ m_{23} \succ m_{22} \succ m_{24};$$
$$m_{32} \succ m_{34} \succ m_{33} \succ m_{31}.$$

And then the corresponding criteria should be reordered according to it in order to compute weights. Therefore, their corresponding criteria can be reordered as follows:

$$C_3, C_4, C_2, C_1;$$
$$C_1, C_3, C_2, C_4;$$
$$C_2, C_4, C_3, C_1.$$

Based on the criteria set $\{C_1, C_2, C_3, C_4\}$ and its predefined fuzzy measure μ, the results of $A^i_{\sigma(j)} \triangleq \{C_{\sigma(1)}, \ldots, C_{\sigma(j)}\}$ and $\psi\left(\mu\left(A^i_{\sigma(j)}\right)\right)$ are shown in Table 1.1 within $A^i_{\sigma(0)} = \varnothing$ for all $j = 1,2,3,4$, $i = 1,2,3$.

c) Let $\quad \psi(x) = \begin{cases} 0 & \text{if } x \leq 0.3; \\ 2(x-0.3) & \text{if } 0.3 < x \leq 0.8; \\ 1 & \text{otherwise,} \end{cases} \quad \text{for } x \in [0, \quad 1]$

then the criteria weights for each alternative based on $\omega^i_j = \psi\left(\mu\left(A^i_{\sigma(j)}\right)\right) - \psi\left(\mu\left(A^i_{\sigma(j-1)}\right)\right)$ are obtained as follows:

$$\omega^1_1 = 0, \ \omega^1_2 = 0.8, \ \omega^1_3 = 0.2, \ \omega^1_4 = 0;$$
$$\omega^2_1 = 0, \ \omega^2_2 = 0.36, \ \omega^2_3 = 0.54, \ \omega^2_4 = 0.1;$$
$$\omega^3_1 = 0.2, \ \omega^3_2 = 0.8, \ \omega^3_3 = 0, \ \omega^3_4 = 0.$$

ii. The ELICIT-Choquet-OWA operator is applied to each alternative to fuse TrFNs and obtain the result $\tilde{\beta}_i = T^i\left(a_i, b_i, c_i, d_i\right)$ for all $i = 1,2,3$ as follows:

$$\tilde{\beta}_1 = T^1\left(0.525, 0.65, 0.675, 0.8\right);$$
$$\tilde{\beta}_2 = T^2\left(0.6125, 0.6813, 0.8163, 0.93\right);$$
$$\tilde{\beta}_3 = T^3\left(0.6025, 0.7275, 0.7275, 0.8\right).$$

TABLE 1.1
Computing Result of $A^i_{\sigma(j)}$ and $\psi\left(\mu\left(A^i_{\sigma(j)}\right)\right)$

		$A^i_{\sigma(1)}$	$A^i_{\sigma(2)}$	$A^i_{\sigma(3)}$	$A^i_{\sigma(4)}$
A_i	$i = 1$	$\{C_3\}$	$\{C_3, C_4\}$	$\{C_3, C_4, C_2\}$	$\{C_1, C_2, C_3, C_4\}$
	$i = 2$	$\{C_1\}$	$\{C_1, C_3\}$	$\{C_1, C_3, C_2\}$	$\{C_1, C_2, C_3, C_4\}$
	$i = 3$	$\{C_2\}$	$\{C_4, C_2\}$	$\{C_4, C_2, C_3\}$	$\{C_1, C_2, C_3, C_4\}$
		$\psi\left(\mu\left(A^i_{\sigma(1)}\right)\right)$	$\psi\left(\mu\left(A^i_{\sigma(2)}\right)\right)$	$\psi\left(\mu\left(A^i_{\sigma(3)}\right)\right)$	$\psi\left(\mu\left(A^i_{\sigma(4)}\right)\right)$
A_i	$i = 1$	0	0.8	1	1
	$i = 2$	0	0.36	0.9	1
	$i = 3$	0.2	1	1	1

iii. The ranking method (Abbasbandy & Hajjari, 2009; Dat, Yu, & Chou, 2012; Dombi & Jónás, 2020; Vincent & Dat, 2014; Wang et al., 2006b; Yager, 1978) of TrFNs is used in order to obtain the best alternative/s as a solution to this MCDM problem.

Here, we use the centroid point $\left(x_0 \left(\tilde{\beta}_i \right), y_0 \left(\tilde{\beta}_i \right) \right)$ of a TrFN $\tilde{\beta}_i$ for all $i = 1, 2, 3$ and its ranking value (RV) introduced in Wang et al. (2006) as follows:

$$x_0 \left(\tilde{\beta}_i \right) = \frac{1}{3} \left[a_i + b_i + c_i + d_i - \frac{d_i c_i - a_i b_i}{\left(d_i + c_i \right) - \left(a_i + b_i \right)} \right];$$

$$y_0 \left(\tilde{\beta}_i \right) = \frac{1}{3} \left[1 - \frac{c_i - b_i}{\left(d_i + c_i \right) - \left(a_i + b_i \right)} \right]; \tag{1.30}$$

$$RV \left(\tilde{\beta}_i \right) = \sqrt{\left(x_0 \left(\tilde{\beta}_i \right) \right)^2 + \left(x_0 \left(\tilde{\beta}_i \right) \right)^2}.$$

Thence, we compute the ranking values and the ranking order of $\tilde{\beta}_i$ as

$$RV \left(\tilde{\beta}_1 \right) = 2.0109; RV \left(\tilde{\beta}_2 \right) = 2.2965; RV \left(\tilde{\beta}_3 \right) = 2.2078.$$

Therefore, $\tilde{\beta}_1 \prec \tilde{\beta}_3 \prec \tilde{\beta}_2$. Accordingly, $\mathcal{A}_1 \prec \mathcal{A}_3 \prec \mathcal{A}_2$.

(3) The ordered TrFNs are retranslated using the function ζ to obtain the final ELICIT expression as shown in Table 1.2.

Step 3: Based on the ranking of TrFNs, that is, $\mathcal{A}_1 \prec \mathcal{A}_3 \prec \mathcal{A}_2$, we select the top 1 alternative $\mathcal{A}_2$ as the solution to this MCDM problem.

TABLE 1.2
Collective ELICIT Expressions

Alternative	Collective ELICIT Expressions $\zeta \left(\tilde{\beta}_i \right)$
$\mathcal{A}_1$	between $(S_5, 0.2)^0$ and $(S_5, 0.4)^0$
$\mathcal{A}_2$	between $(S_5, 0.4504)^{0.0035}$ and $(S_7, -0.4696)^{-0.00070625}$
$\mathcal{A}_3$	$(S_6, -0.18)^0$

1.7 CONCLUSIONS

This contribution aims to address the resolution of MCDM problems considering the interactions between criteria in the context of ELICIT information for modeling experts' preferences.

Obviously, the interrelationship between the criteria is not easy to capture because it is inherently ambiguous and uncertain. In this sense, the Choquet integral models such uncertainty through the definition of a nonadditive fuzzy measure and captures the interaction among different elements. On the other hand, the OWA aggregation operator has been widely and successfully used for carrying out aggregation processes in MCDM under fuzzy contexts. However, it is not able to consider the relation between criteria in the aggregation.

Therefore, we have combined the OWA operator with the Choquet integral to fuse ELICIT information, proposing the so-called ELICIT-Choquet-OWA operator, which is able to aggregate ELICIT information by using an OWA operator whose weights are derived from the Choquet integral. In addition, we have proposed a new model based on the proposed operator for solving MCDM problems. Finally, its practicality and feasibility have been illustrated in a case study.

In the future, we will study other classical operators combined with the Choquet integral to deal with large-scale group decision making with ELICIT information. It can be applied to the consensus reaching process or minimum cost consensus models.

REFERENCES

Abbasbandy, S., & Hajjari, T. (2009). A new approach for ranking of trapezoidal fuzzy numbers. *Computers & Mathematics with Applications*, *57* (3), 413–419.

Ali, Z., Mahmood, T., & Yang, M.-S. (2020). TOPSIS method based on complex spherical fuzzy sets with Bonferroni mean operators. *Mathematics*, *8* (10), 1739.

Almutairi, K., Hosseini Dehshiri, S. J., Hosseini Dehshiri, S. S., Mostafaeipour, A., Hoa, A. X., & Techato, K. (2022). Determination of optimal renewable energy growth strategies using swot analysis, hybrid MCDM methods, and game theory: A case study. *International Journal of Energy Research*, *46* (5), 6766–6789.

Cables, E., Lamata, M., & Verdegay, J. (2016). Rim-reference ideal method in multicriteria decision making. *Information Sciences*, *337–338*, 1–10.

Chen, L., Duan, G., Wang, S., & Ma, J. (2020). A Choquet integral based fuzzy logic approach to solve uncertain multi-criteria decision making problem. *Expert Systems with Applications*, *149*, 113303.

Chen, Z. S., Chin, K. S., & Tsui, K. L. (2019). Constructing the geometric Bonferroni mean from the generalized Bonferroni mean with several extensions to linguistic 2-tuples for decision-making. *Applied Soft Computing*, *78*, 595–613.

Choquet, G. (1954). Theory of capacities. In *Annales de l'institut fourier* (Vol. 5, pp. 131–295).

Dat, L. Q., Yu, V. F., & Chou, S.-Y. (2012). An improved ranking method for fuzzy numbers based on the centroid-index. *International Journal of Fuzzy Systems*, *14* (3), 413–419.

Dombi, J., & Jónás, T. (2020). Ranking trapezoidal fuzzy numbers using a parametric relation pair. *Fuzzy Sets and Systems*, *399*, 20–43.

Dutta, B., Labella, Á., Rodríguez, R. M., & Martínez, L. (2019). Aggregating interrelated attributes in multi-attribute decision-making with ELICIT information based on Bonferroni mean and its variants. *International Journal of Computational Intelligence Systems*, *12* (2), 1179–1196.

Fei, L., Wang, H., Chen, L., & Deng, Y. (2019). A new vector valued similarity measure for intuitionistic fuzzy sets based on OWA operators. *Iranian Journal of Fuzzy Systems*, *16* (3), 113–126.

García-Zamora, D., Labella, Á., Rodríguez, R. M., & Martínez, L. (2022). A linguistic metric for consensus reaching processes based on ELICIT comprehensive minimum cost consensus models. *IEEE Transactions on Fuzzy Systems*, 1–13. doi: 10.1109/ TFUZZ.2022.3213943

Garg, A., Maiti, J., & Kumar, A. (2022). Granulized Z-OWA aggregation operator and its application in fuzzy risk assessment. *International Journal of Intelligent Systems*, *37* (2), 1479–1508.

Grabisch, M., & Roubens, M. (2000). Application of the Choquet integral in multicriteria decision making. *Fuzzy Measures and Integrals-Theory and Applications*, 348–374.

He, W., Dutta, B., Rodríguez, R. M., Alzahrani, A. A., & Martínez, L. (2021a). Induced OWA operator for group decision making dealing with extended comparative linguistic expressions with symbolic translation. *Mathematics*, *9*, 20.

He, W., Dutta, B., Rodríguez, R. M., & Martínez, L. (2021b). Application of Choquet integral operator to aggregate ELICIT information. In *International conference on intelligent and fuzzy systems* (pp. 272–280). doi: 10.1007/978-3-030-85626-733

He, W., Rodríguez, R. M., Dutta, B., & Martínez, L. (2021c). Exploiting the type-1 OWA operator to fuse the elicit information. In *2021 IEEE international conference on fuzzy systems (fuzz-ieee)* (p. 1–7). doi: 10.1109/FUZZ45933.2021.9494400

He, W., Rodríguez, R. M., Dutta, B., & Martínez, L. (2022). A type-1 OWA operator for extended comparative linguistic expressions with symbolic translation. *Fuzzy Sets and Systems*, *446*, 167–192.

Herrera, F., & Martínez, L. (2000a). A 2-tuple fuzzy linguistic representation model for computing with words. *IEEE Transactions on fuzzy systems*, *8* (6), 746–752.

Herrera, F., & Martínez, L. (2000b). A 2-tuple fuzzy linguistic representation model for computing with words. *IEEE Transactions on Fuzzy Systems*, *8* (6), 746–752.

Hussain, W., Merigó, J. M., & Raza, M. R. (2022c). Predictive intelligence using ANFIS-induced OWAWA for complex stock market prediction. *International Journal of Intelligent Systems*, *37* (8), 4586–4611.

Hussain, W., Merigó, J. M., Raza, M. R., & Gao, H. (2022b). A new QoS prediction model using hybrid IOWA-ANFIS with fuzzy C-means, subtractive clustering and grid partitioning. *Information Sciences*, *584*, 280–300.

Hussain, W., Raza, M. R., Jan, M. A., Merigo, J. M., & Gao, H. (2022a). Cloud risk management with OWA-LSTM predictive intelligence and fuzzy linguistic decision making. *IEEE Transactions on Fuzzy Systems*, *30*(11), 4657–4666.

Kabadayi, N., & Dehghanimohammadabadi, M. (2022). Multi-objective supplier selection process: a simulation–optimization framework integrated with MCDM. *Annals of Operations Research*, 1–23, doi: 10.1007/s10479-021-04424-2

Keeny, R., & Raiffa, H. (1976). *Decisions with multiple objectives: Preferences and value tradeoffs*. New York: John Wiley & Sons Inc.

Kumar, A., Singh, P., Kaur, A., & Kaur, P. (2010). Rm approach for ranking of generalized trapezoidal fuzzy numbers. *Fuzzy Information and Engineering*, *2* (1), 37–47.

Labella, Á., Rodríguez, R. M., & Martínez, L. (2019). Computing with comparative linguistic expressions and symbolic translation for decision making: ELICIT information. *IEEE Transactions on Fuzzy Systems*, *28* (10), 2510–2522.

Labella, Á., Rodríguez, R. M., Alzahrani, A. A., & Martínez, L. (2020). A consensus model for extended comparative linguistic expressions with symbolic translation. *Mathematics*, *8* (12), 2198.

Liang, W., & Wang, Y.-M. (2020). Interval-valued hesitant fuzzy stochastic decision-making method based on regret theory. *International Journal of Fuzzy Systems*, *22* (4), 1091–1103.

Meng, F., Chen, S.-M., & Tang, J. (2021). Multicriteria decision making based on bi-direction Choquet integrals. *Information Sciences, 555*, 339–356.

Merigó, J., & Casanovas, M. (2008). Using fuzzy numbers in heavy aggregation operators. *International Journal of Information Technology, 4* (3), 177–182.

Murofushi, T., & Sugeno, M. (1989). An interpretation of fuzzy measures and the Choquet integral as an integral with respect to a fuzzy measure. *Fuzzy Sets and Systems, 29* (2), 201–227.

Rodríguez, R. M., Labella, Á., & Martínez, L. (2016). An overview on fuzzy modelling of complex linguistic preferences in decision making. *International Journal of Computational Intelligence Systems, 9*, 81–94.

Rodríguez, R. M., Martínez, L., & Herrera, F. (2012). Hesitant fuzzy linguistic term sets for decision making. *IEEE Transactions on Fuzzy Systems, 20* (1), 109–119.

Rodríguez, R. M., Martínez, L., & Herrera, F. (2013). A group decision making model dealing with comparative linguistic expressions based on hesitant fuzzy linguistic term sets. *Information Sciences, 241*, 28–42.

Savitha, M., & Mary, G. (2017). New methods for ranking of trapezoidal fuzzy numbers. *Advances in Fuzzy Mathematics, 12* (5), 1159–1170.

Sugeno, M. (1993). Fuzzy measures and fuzzy integrals—a survey. In *Readings in fuzzy sets for intelligent systems* (pp. 251–257). San Francisco: Elsevier.

Tang, Y., & Zheng, J. (2006). Linguistic modelling based on semantic similarity relation among linguistic labels. *Fuzzy Sets and Systems, 157* (12), 1662–1673.

Uluta, S. A., Stanujkic, D., Karabasevic, D., Popovic, G., Zavadskas, E. K., Smarandache, F., & Brauers, W. K. (2021). Developing of a novel integrated MCDM multimoosral approach for supplier selection. *Informatica, 32* (1), 145–161.

Vincent, F. Y., & Dat, L. Q. (2014). An improved ranking method for fuzzy numbers with integral values. *Applied Soft Computing, 14*, 603–608.

Wang, J.-H., & Hao, J. (2006). A new version of 2-tuple fuzzy linguistic representation model for computing with words. *IEEE Transactions on Fuzzy Systems, 14* (3), 435–445.

Wang, Y., & Deng, Y. (2019). OWA aggregation of multi-criteria with mixed uncertain fuzzy satisfactions. *arXiv preprint arXiv:1901.09784*.

Wang, Y.-M., Yang, J.-B., & Xu, D.-L. (2006b). Environmental impact assessment using the evidential reasoning approach. *European Journal of Operational Research, 174* (3), 1885–1913.

Wang, Y.-M., Yang, J.-B., Xu, D.-L., & Chin, K.-S. (2006a). On the centroids of fuzzy numbers. *Fuzzy Sets and Systems, 157* (7), 919–926.

Yager, R. R. (1978). Ranking fuzzy subsets over the unit interval. In *1978 IEEE conference on decision and control including the 17th symposium on adaptive processes* (pp. 1435–1437). doi: 10.1109/CDC.1978.268154

Yager, R. R. (1988). On ordered weighted averaging aggregation operators in multicriteria decision making. *IEEE Transactions on Systems, Man, and Cybernetics, 18* (1), 183–190.

Yager, R. R. (1996). Quantifier guided aggregation using OWA operators. *International Journal of Intelligent Systems, 11* (1), 49–73.

Yager, R. R. (2008). Using trapezoids for representing granular objects: Applications to learning and OWA aggregation. *Information Sciences, 178* (2), 363–380.

Zadeh, L. A. (1965). Fuzzy sets. *Information and Control, 8* (3), 338–353.

Zadeh, L. A. (1975a). The concept of a linguistic variable and its application to approximate reasoning—III. *Information Sciences, 9* (1), 43–80.

Zadeh, L. A. (1975b). The concept of a linguistic variable and its application to approximate reasoning—I. *Information Sciences, 8* (3), 199–249.

Zadeh, L. A. (1975c). The concept of a linguistic variable and its application to approximate reasoning—II. *Information Sciences, 8* (4), 301–357.

Zarghami, M., Szidarovszky, F., & Ardakanian, R. (2008). A fuzzy stochastic OWA model for robust multi-criteria decision making. *Fuzzy Optimization and Decision Making, 7*, 1–15.

2 GPipe
Using Adaptive Directed Acyclic Graphs to Run Data and Feature Pipelines with on-the-fly Transformations

José Hélio de Brum Müller
Private consultant, Sydney, Australia

Fethi Rabhi
UNSW, Sydney, Australia

Zoran Milosevic
Deontik, Australia
Institute for Integrated and Intelligent Systems,
Griffith University, Nathan, Australia

2.1 INTRODUCTION

Every day huge amounts of data are produced and processed for decision making via reporting, data analysis and ML systems. Traditional data engineering methods extract data from many data sources, transform it and load it into several layers. Such a process has become widely known as ETL, a type of data pipeline defined by a sequential processing of tasks, implemented and maintained by data engineers. Businesses gain significant value from data for decision making via data analytics and assessing reports created by business intelligence tools such as Tableau and Power BI. The data is also used by data scientists to train ML models that help businesses in making predictions, recommendations, etc.

We define *raw data* as the data generated by applications and users and scattered in different data sources (databases, files, etc.). As raw data comes in many different formats, it is the responsibility of data engineers to connect, clean and organize it in a certain structure and format that it can be easily used by data analysts and data scientists. This work is done by applying transformations via scripts (e.g., using SQL, Python Pandas, Scala or PySpark) that read raw data from different sources, aggregate, clean, transform and save it back into tables. As an example of a transformation, country codes AU, USA and BR are transformed into country names Australia, the United States of America and Brazil.

DOI: 10.1201/9781003340621-2

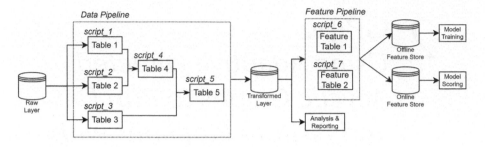

FIGURE 2.1   Data and feature pipeline.

Most of the tables generated by the data pipeline are used by data and business analysts for analysis and reporting. In addition, data scientists create feature tables containing feature data by implementing other scripts that generate and aggregate feature tables in a feature store, usually an offline feature store[1] that is used to train ML models. This process is called feature engineering and we are defining this sequence of processes as a feature pipeline as shown on the right of Figure 2.1.

Once data scientists finish model training, the model is published to serve application requests, that is, a model scoring phase. In this phase, features, usually historical data, are already saved in the online feature store[2] (Figure 2.1); other features, usually derived from non-historical data, must be transformed on the fly to be used by ML models which require mapping and, sometimes, recoding all transformations back to the raw data sources.

There are many solutions for this problem that are discussed in Section 2.2. However, the following challenges still need to be addressed:

1. Dependencies change management: How to avoid for the data engineer the manual management of several dependencies in the pipeline as complexity increases with size and in the presence of frequent changes?
2. How can the data scientist map all dependencies from features to raw data without reverse engineering?
3. How to maintain an efficient implementation by only performing partial processing of the data that are impacted by changes?
4. How to maintain data and feature pipelines portable and more platform agnostic?
5. How to minimize infrastructure cost and complexity to run on-the-fly transformations?

In this chapter, we propose a new technique that uses DAGs for distributing and delegating an individual script's responsibility into smaller scripts, herein called as transformers. Each one of these smaller scripts will generate one or few columns rather than full tables, and each transformer will be responsible to import its dependencies (other transformers) and apply the transformations. Therefore, a table script will become a mere aggregator of these smaller scripts. In this way, maintenance and changes in any column transformation are propagated throughout the pipelines and coding is simplified as engineers can focus on less number of codes and be more dedicated and define a logic of a column.

Section 2.2 presents the background and related work. Section 2.3 describes our solution and Section 2.4 describes our implementation with experimental results. Section 2.5 concludes this paper.

2.2   BACKGROUND AND RELATED WORK

The most common way to implement data pipelines is to schedule and monitor tasks using workflow orchestrator platforms, for example, Apache Airflow [1] that periodically trigger transformations as programmed by data engineers. These processes are executed in platforms optimized for data analysis and engineering, and ML, such as Databricks [2], see Figure 2.2.

Script dependencies are usually expressed using a DAG. Changes in scripts can cause downstream failures in the pipeline such as when adding new scripts but forgetting to set up some dependencies in the orchestrator or removing (or renaming) columns but not updating the corresponding scripts. These failures are quite hard to avoid as data engineers do not know beforehand what metadata changes will impact subsequent scripts. The workaround is to manually search for all posterior-dependent DAGs and scripts and assess the impact of the changes on each one of them.

Another problem is that because some applications require model scoring as quickly as possible, businesses store these features in online feature stores with low-latency responses. However, there are features that need to be created on-the-fly as data has just been created. For example, suppose a company that needs to call a model to predict the probability of default of a loan application to decide if it can be accepted or not, some historical features can be retrieved from an online feature store such as customers' number of default contracts with the company, but other features like requested loan amount would have just been created by the application and therefore are not in the feature store. Data streams [3] are one of the most common options to transform and load data on the fly. Solutions like Databricks Structured Streaming [4] can be used together with Apache Kafka [5] for live data and feature transformations with ~100 ms at best; for lower latencies, Spark [6] published an experimental Continuous Processing [7] that enables low (~1 ms) end-to-end latency. Figure 2.3 shows an example of on-the-fly transformation, where systems publish events containing raw data to Apache Kafka that notifies Databricks to create features and return the model predictions.

Despite these solutions having low latency, some challenges yet persist. First, the use of the same scripts from the pipelines, depicted in (Figure 2.1), for this purpose is not feasible because these scripts generate tables and require all preceding data, which can easily increase the payload in stream events, overload the service and slowdown the processing due to network traffic. At this point, one option would be to reverse engineer all those scripts back to raw data, extract and re-implement only the logic necessary again to recreate the features. However, as this process repeats over each model and feature, it will increase the development and maintenance costs as the logics are replicated and it will be even more challenging to implement big and complex transformations and also not be trustworthy as the re-implemented pipeline transformations can differ from the stream transformations. Further, there is the overhead of maintaining more complex streaming and message service infrastructure and most of the cases are out of reach to companies with less resources.

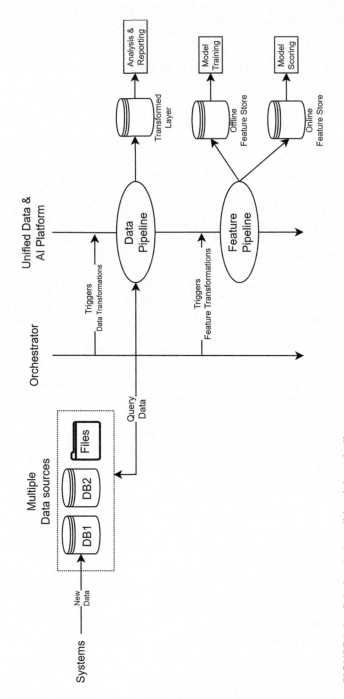

FIGURE 2.2   Solution A: A traditional data pipeline.

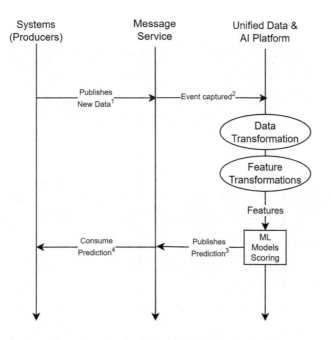

FIGURE 2.3   Solution B: Data and feature transformation using message service (i.e., Kafka) and Unified Data & AI Platform (i.e., Databricks), where

1. Systems, acting as producers, publish a new event with the data to be transformed into a message.
2. Systems, acting as consumers, subscribe to the message service and are notified of events to retrieve the message (create features and do model scoring).
3. Same consumers publish a new event with the prediction.
4. Systems are notified and retrieve the prediction.

A hybrid solution (illustrated in Figure 2.4) would consist of separating historical features (previously pre-computed and ingested into online feature stores) and re-coding of specific features for on-the-fly transformation.

However, these hybrid approaches become challenging if not impossible because teams start duplicating the codes of these transformations in Spark (i.e., using PySpark) and non-Spark environments, say Python and Pandas. Now teams face problems in not only having to duplicate codes but also in maintaining codes in different syntaxes.

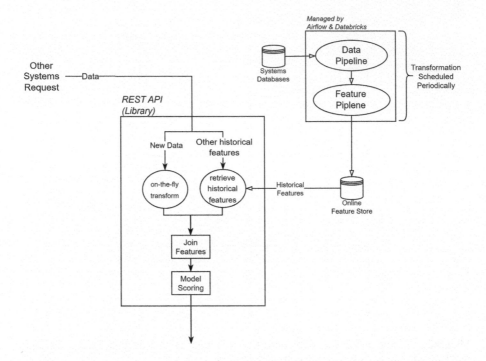

FIGURE 2.4   Solution C: Hybrid transformation using on-the-fly transformations and online features for low-latency systems.

TABLE 2.1
Challenges and Popular Market Solutions

Challenge	Solution Traditional Pipelines	Message Services	Hybrid Transformations
Dependencies management	Manual	Scattered in duplicated logic	Scattered in duplicated logic
Dependencies mapping	Reverse engineering	Reverse engineering	Reverse engineering
Partial processing	Only on table level	Tables and message level	Tables and libraries
Platform agnostic	Tied to the environment	Tied to multiple environments	Tied to multiple environments
Infrastructure cost and complexity	Less complex; don't support on-the-fly transformation	More complex; on-the-fly transformation needs re-implementation	More complex; on-the-fly transformation needs re-implementation

2.3 PROPOSED SOLUTION

2.3.1 MOTIVATING EXAMPLE

A company has developed a prediction model with several features built on top of tables generated by the traditional data pipeline and each table is generated by different scripts. When deploying the model, they realized that most of the features were dependent on the newly created data by the customers but the existing pipeline that generates the features was scheduled to run daily. Therefore, they need a faster way of re-creating these features to allow online predictions to retrieve faster answers back to the customers. At this point, a hybrid solution was decided and they started reverse engineering by mapping all data transformations from data sources to features.

The dependency graph is illustrated in Figure 2.5 which shows that the model requires logical extraction of features f_{11}, f_{12} and f_{21} and all required preceding transformations, implemented in multiple dependent scripts (challenge 2).

2.3.2 REPRESENTING DATA AND FEATURE TRANSFORMATIONS USING A DAG

This idea is breaking the implementation of the pipeline into modular scripts operating, whenever possible, at the column (not table) level. For this, each object t_{ij} will be responsible for extracting the raw data necessary to create column j of table I, and a third object will be created to join the outputs of t_{ij} into a table, see Figure 2.6.

For example, to capture the transformations shown in the pipeline defined in Figure 2.5, we can build a DAG that considers all dependencies between transformations, feature transformations, tables and feature tables; see Figure 2.7.

This graph allows the calculation of any column independent of the table in which it will be residing. In this example, we only need to process ten transformations t_{11}, t_{12}, t_{22}, t_{31}, t_{42}, t_{52}, f_{11}, f_{12}, f_{21} and FM_1 instead of 17 transformations (all tables and FM_1) as shown in Figure 2.5. It can be reduced to only one process (FM_1), if f_{11}, f_{12} and f_{21} are cached, as discussed in Section 2.3.3.

2.3.3 PROCESSING DAGS

As there can be hundreds of tables with dozens of columns each, if features are dependent on the traditional data pipelines, the number of processes to generate features for models will grow proportionally to the number of columns in each dependent table and the number of processes to calculate FM_1 will be:

$$number_{processed} = 1 + number_{dependent\ tables} * number_{columns\ of\ dependent\ tables} \qquad (2.1)$$

However, the number of transformations in this new technique will be constant (e.g., ten processes in the above example) as nodes are processed independent of the pipeline.

Figure 2.8 demonstrates how the graph can be simplified. The logic to process node FM_1 or any other node is to process in parallel nodes with an in-degree[3] of 0,

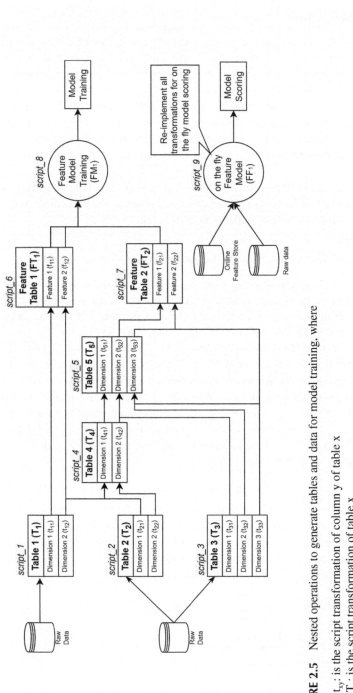

FIGURE 2.5 Nested operations to generate tables and data for model training, where

- t_{xy}: is the script transformation of column y of table x
- T_x: is the script transformation of table x
- f_{xy}: is the script transformation of feature y of feature table x
- FM_x (feature model transformer): is the script transformation to create training and test data to train model x
- Model training: is the script to train an ML model
- FF_x (on-the-fly feature transformer): is the script transformation to re-create features on the fly for model x

FM1 script where the data is sliced in training, test and validation data, scalers and encoders as created and applied to the data. FR1 script where on-the-fly transformations are re-implemented, usually connected to online feature stores and other data sources (databases, Rest APIs, etc.).

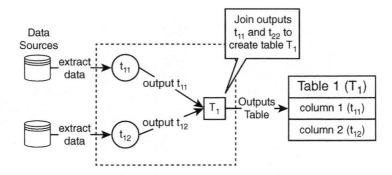

FIGURE 2.6 Table T1 creation by isolating transformations t_{11} and t_{22}.

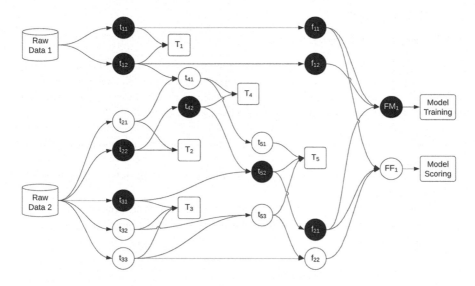

FIGURE 2.7 DAG to process data and feature transformations.

collect the outputs, remove these nodes from the graph, process next nodes with an in-degree of 0 and repeat until FM_1 is processed.

If FM_1 is triggered many times (say implementation phase), unnecessary processing resources will be continuously used, slowing down the development. To save resources and time, nodes f_{11}, f_{22} and f_{21} can be cached as the outputs $fout_{11}$, $fout_{12}$ and $fout_{21}$ are the only data needed to process FM_1.

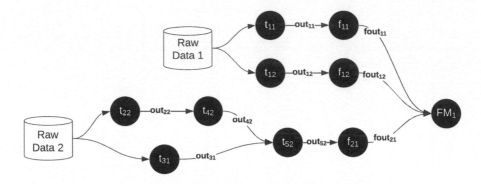

FIGURE 2.8   FM1 processing graph.

2.4   EVALUATION

2.4.1   Prototype Implementation

This section describes a prototype implementation of the proposed framework using the Python language [8], a PostgreSQL database and the public dataset "Breakfast at the Frat" provided by dunnhumby [9]. The role of the framework is creating and managing transformation dependencies via DAGs, where

1. Each transformation can be triggered independently via cached results from the preceding transformations.
2. Each transformation can have its own unit tests and is independent of the preceding transformations.
3. Transformations will be implemented using Pandas dataframes.[4]
4. Transformations can be packaged, installed and used under Spark or non-Spark environments.

The design of the prototype consists of six modules:

1. **GPipe:** For mapping and creating the DAG.
2. **Cache:** Saves the running time of each node and retrieves cached results.
3. **Transformers:** Applies the transformation and defines the input and output metadata.
4. **Publishers:** Aggregates transformations and saves them into a table.
5. **Pipeline:** Aggregates multiple publishers.
6. **Data Source:** Connects and retrieves data from a data source.

Each module is now described in turn. A UML diagram showing the relationships between these modules is illustrated in Figure 2.9.

2.4.1.1   Transformers Module

Defines the logic of a node and its dependencies in the DAG. The transformation can be implemented using syntaxes like Python Pandas or PySpark dataframe. This class

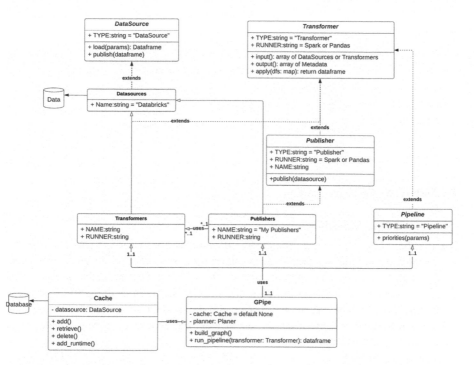

FIGURE 2.9 An UML diagram of prototype implementation.

defines dependencies, joins inputs, applies transformations and outputs a dataframe according to the metadata defined. It is composed of three methods:

1. **Input**: Returns an array of other transformers or data sources that the trans- former is dependent on.
2. **Output**: Returns an array of metadata defining what columns and data types that the transformer outputs.
3. **Apply**: After the framework collects the input dataframe defined in the *input* method and retrieves a dictionary of dataframes, this method applies trans- formations and returns a dataframe that must match the metadata defined in the *output* method.

2.4.1.2   Publishers Module

It is an extension of transformers that joins outputs from other transformers and knows how to save the results into a table.

2.4.1.3   Pipeline Module

It is an extension of transformers, and it is used for aggregating multiple transformers into a single graph to be processed. It is used as a helper class to aggregate multiple DAGs into a single DAG.

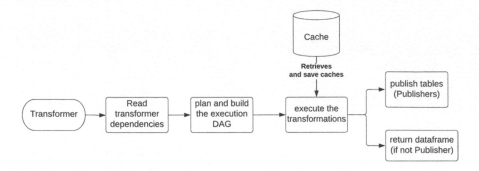

FIGURE 2.10   GPipe process flow.

2.4.1.4   GPipe Module

This is the main class of the framework. It receives a transformer and controls the processing of the pipeline, builds the graph and plans the execution; see Figure 2.10.

As each transformer is implemented by defining its dependencies implemented inside method *input*, it allows building of a routine that creates the graph to process a specific transformer. We now describe the method *build_graph* of the module GPipe that builds the DAG necessary to process the given *transformer* (instance of *Transformer*) and its predecessors.

The object *transformer* can be any node in Figure 2.7 (T_1, f_{11}, t_{51}, FM_1, etc.). Assuming FM_1 is given as an argument to *build_graph*, it will be initially added to the graph and then each transformer defined in the method *input* of FM_1 (f_{11}, f_{12} and f_{21}) will be added to the graph with directed edges to FM_1 (f_{11}–FM_1, f_{12}–FM1 and f_{21}–FM_1); subsequently, if the node output has not been cached (processed or given by the user), then it is invoked recursively by calling self.build_graph(input) which will repeat the process and add dependent transformers to the graph until data sources are reached.

This ability to process any transformer in the graph together with the use of caches is what allows any partial processing of the graph. It is very useful for the development and implementation of unit tests and the re-use of the same pipeline for on-the-fly transformation. The *build_graph* method can be expressed in pseudo-code as follows:

```
def build_graph(self, transformer: Transformer):
  self.add_node(transformer)

  if transformer.type == "Data Source":
    return transformer

  for input in transformer.input():
    self.add_node(input)
    self.graph.add_edge(input, transformer)

    if self._has_cache(input):
      self.cache.add(input)
```

```
    else:
       self.build_graph(input)

  return transformer
```

In this DAG building process, many transformers can refer to the same data source and table, but with different columns. The method *add_node* (part of the GPipe module and invoked by *build_graph*) will aggregate all these columns required by the graph into a single query, keeping the number of queries to the data source to a minimum, as demonstrated in the following code.

```
def add_node(self, transformer: Transformer):

  if transformer.type == "Data Source" and \
     self.graph.has_node(transformer):
     node = self.graph.get_node(transformer)
     node.columns = set(node.columns
                          + transformer.columns)
     self.graph.update_node(node)

  elif not self.graph.has_node(transformer):
     self.graph.add_node(transformer)
```

Once the graph is built, the execution process starts by invoking the method *run_pipeline*. This method will process in parallel all nodes with an in-degree of 0, cache the outputs, remove these nodes from the graph and continue the process until all nodes up to the transformer (in our example, FM_1) have been processed, as shown in the following code:

```
def run_pipeline(self, transformer: Transformer):

  while self.graph.has_nodes():
     for node in self.graph.get_nodes(in_degree=0):

        if node == transformer:
           return node.apply_transformation()
        else:
           self.add_queue_parallel_processing(node,
              cache_results=True)
```

2.4.2 EXPERIMENTAL RESULTS

We built a simple graph pipeline for the dataset "Breakfast at the Frat" that contains three tables: Product (58 records), Store (79 records) and Transaction (524950 records). The graph builds a star schema of two-dimensional tables DimStore and DimProduct and one fact table FactSale. It was created using an extra transformation

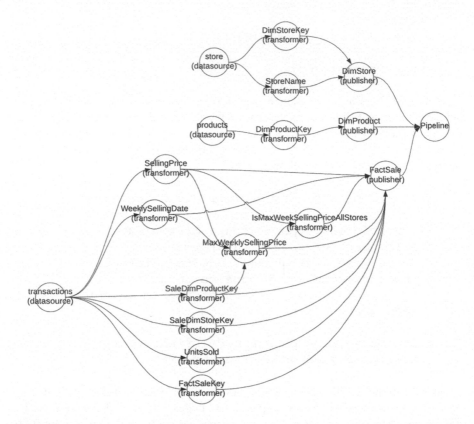

FIGURE 2.11   "Breakfast at the Frat" pipeline graph to build tables DimStore, DimProduct and FactSale.

IsMaxWeeklySellingPriceAll that tags product sales in the FactSale table if the sale has the maximum selling price of each product in all stores. Figure 2.11 represents the DAG of this dataset.

We ran the pipeline 100 times recreating the tables DimStore, DimProduct and FactSale using no cached outputs of each node and using cached outputs. Table 2.2 shows the average running time of each transformation.

The use of caching to compute more expensive nodes, like IsMaxWeekly SellingPriceAll, can speed up the processing. However, the use of caching may not be the best strategy if there are multiple caches to be retrieved by the database, for example, FactSale and MaxWeeklySellingPrice. The use of caches can be convenient when debugging during development if the dependent nodes are too expensive to be continuously re-processed.

TABLE 2.2

Average Running Time of 100 Runs Using Cached and Non-cached Nodes Outputs

Transformer	No Cache (sec)	Using Cache (sec)	Faster (>0.4 sec)
FactSale	5.446	9.129	No cache (3.68 sec)
FeatureModel	3.691	4.009	–
MaxWeeklySellingPrice	2.859	3.799	No cache (0.94 sec)
IsMaxWeeklySellingPriceAll	2.863	2.369	Cache (0.5 sec)
FactSaleKey	1.534	1.929	–
WeekSellingDate	1.136	1.153	–
SellingPrice	1.056	1.081	–
SalesDimProductKey	0.964	0.963	–
ProductUniqueBaskets	0.912	0.904	–
SalesDimStoreKey	0.919	0.901	–
UnitsSold	0.893	0.883	–
DimStoreKey	0.69	0.072	–
StoreName	0.072	0.07	–
DimProductKey	0.069	0.069	–
DimStore	0.073	0.016	–
DimProduct	0.073	0.011	–

2.5   CONCLUSIONS AND FUTURE WORK

In summary, the work proposes a framework to address the challenges associated with implementing and maintaining data and feature pipelines being used for multiple purposes (e.g., reporting and making real-time predictions) within a large organization. The proposed solution addressed the challenges (listed in Table 2.1) as follows:

- **Dependencies mapping:** As all dependencies are defined inside transformers, it is easier to automatically map dependencies, evaluate the impact of changes in the metadata of any specific node in the downstream pipeline and without executing the pipeline, save development time and resources. It is also possible to map all raw data sources (tables and columns) required to process any node by recursively visiting antecessors until data sources.
- **Infrastructure cost and complexity:** If transformations are implemented using Pandas syntax, it is possible to package the whole data and feature pipelines into a single Python library that can be used for on-the-fly transformation in non-Spark environments, say Rest APIs, without more complex streaming infrastructure.
- **Partial Processing:** In situations where results from predecessors are cached or given, say via Rest APIs or unit tests, the whole processing time can be considerably reduced as only a part of the graph is used to re-generate features, useful for on-the-fly transformations.
- **Platform agnostic:** If transformations are implemented using Pandas syntax, the same graph can be processed under Spark environments using Pandas on Spark or non-Spark environments, using traditional Python Pandas.

The main limitation is that we have only considered in our implementation a small dataset. Further work is in progress[5] to process larger databases containing more records and tables to better represent big data environments where processing can be more expensive when running all dependent nodes. In addition, our implementation did not use Spark environments as they can have a higher latency when retrieving data from data sources and applying transformations compared to using Pandas dataframes and PostgreSQL. Since Spark can process big volumes of data and has more capability in caching results for further processing, further investigations are needed for better use of automatic caching in pipelines (multiple dataframes).

Finally, the integration of streaming capabilities within the proposed solution, taking into account previous work on low-latency real-time solutions, needs to be investigated [13, 14].

NOTES

1 Store of a large volume of features for training ML models that do not require low latency, shall not be used for live predictions and can contain unstable or in-development features.
2 Contain pre-calculated and ready-to-use features accessed by online model scoring, usually stored in low-latency databases such as PostgreSQL, MSSql, MySQL, etc.
3 In-degree is the number of dependent and non-processed transformations of a node.
4 It can be implemented in PySpark (PySpark Dataframes [10], Spark SQL [11] or pandas on spark [12]) Preference to use pandas on Spark as the same code with pandas like syntax will run under non-Spark environment (Pandas Dataframe) and on-Spark environment (pandas on Spark), but this will be later converted into Spark operations in the backend. Therefore, the pipeline will be portable across Spark and non-Spark environments.
5 Public Python library is available at https://github.com/flypipe/flypipe

REFERENCES

1. Apache Airflow, https://airflow.apache.org/docs/apache-airflow/stable/index.html, last accessed 2022/06/08.
2. Databricks, https://databricks.com/, last accessed 2022/06/08.
3. Pigni, F. et al.: Digital Data Streams: Creating Value from the Real-Time Flow of Big Data. *California Management Review* Vol. 58, no. 3 (2016).
4. Armbrust, M. et al.: Structured Streaming: A Declarative API for Real-Time Applications in Apache Spark. In: *SIGMOD'18: 2018 International Conference on Management of Data*, pp. 601–612, Houston, TX, USA (2018).
5. Apache Kafka, https://kafka.apache.org/intro, last accessed 2022/04/18.
6. Apache Spark, https://spark.apache.org/docs/latest/, last accessed 2022/04/18.
7. Spark Continuous Processing, https://spark.apache.org/docs/latest/structured-streaming-programming-guide.html#continuous-processing, last accessed 2022/06/08.
8. Crickard, P.: *Data Engineering with Python: Work with Massive Datasets to Design Data Models and Automate Data Pipelines Using Python* Birmingham: Packt Publishing, Limited (2020).
9. Public Dataset Breakfast at the Frat Provided by dunnhumby, https://www.dunnhumby.com/source-files, last accessed 2022/05/15.
10. PySpark Dataframes, https://spark.apache.org/docs/latest/api/python/reference/api/pyspark.sql.DataFrame.html, last accessed 2022/06/08.
11. Spark SQL, https://spark.apache.org/sql/, last accessed 2022/06/08.

12. Pandas on Spark, https://databricks.com/blog/2021/10/04/pandas-api-on-upcoming-apache-spark-3-2.html, last accessed 2022/06/08.
13. Luong, N.N.T., Milosevic, Z., Berry, A., Rabhi, F.A.: An Open Architecture for Complex Event Processing with Machine Learning. In: *EDOC*, Eindhoven, Netherlands, pp. 51–56 (2020).
14. Milosevic, Z., Chen, W., Berry, A., Rabhi, F.A.: An Open Architecture for Event-Based Analytics. *International Journal of Data Science and Analytics* Vol. 2, no. 1, 13–27 (2016).

3 Building an ESG Decision-Making System
Challenges and Research Directions

Fethi Rabhi, Mingqin Yu, Alan Ng, Eric Lim and Felix Tan
University of New South Wales, Sydney, Australia

Alan Hsiao
Cognitivo, Sydney, Australia

3.1 INTRODUCTION

Environment, social and governance (ESG) has gained prominence in recent years due to several governments and international organizations pushing for the adoption of various ESG goals and regulations. Besides having a profound impact on social and economic lives worldwide, many IT-related challenges are associated with such changes, which require the academic community to undertake new research studies. In particular, there is a need to investigate adequate information processing and distribution infrastructures that can assist organizations in supporting their ESG goals and meeting their compliance requirements.

As many countries become signatories of international accords and introduce new ESG legislations, many organizations ask questions such as: will this result in new requirements for changing established corporate governance and reporting processes? Will it require a different IT infrastructure to support these requirements? Can I reuse all or part of my existing IT assets? How can we trust internal and external data? How can we support broadening ESG measures, such as the governance of AI, software supply chain and other emerging tech risks? etc.

Defining the scope of appropriate research studies and the expertise needed to deliver tangible outcomes for the industry is difficult as ESG is not well understood and tends to be perceived from one particular discipline-specific lens or to be amalgamated with other areas. Therefore, ESG-related challenges should be tackled as a multidisciplinary collaboration between different academic disciplines (e.g. computing, information systems, business, risk management and compliance).

DOI: 10.1201/9781003340621-3

More specifically, existing information management practices that tend to be qualitative have shown many limitations, leading to high costs and inaccuracies. We believe there are many opportunities to exploit the power of digital transformation technologies and big data analytics to create new ways to support emerging ESG-related activities in data collection, data processing, compliance checking, trusted analytics etc. In other words, we need new research efforts aimed at supporting organizations in meeting their ESG goals from a quantitative rather than a qualitative perspective. Although ESG is a global phenomenon, our report will primarily use the Australian context to illustrate ESG challenges and discuss possible use cases that will provide the type of research projects that are needed as part of a new research agenda in the area of ESG.

The rest of this chapter is structured as follows. Section 3.2 describes the ESG background and the terminology used in this chapter, giving examples of ESG goals and regulations. Section 3.3 describes the ESG data lifecycle and the IT-related challenges that need to be addressed in building and managing complex data processing pipelines. Section 3.4 describes some research areas that could provide the basis for addressing these challenges. Section 3.5 concludes this chapter.

3.2   ESG BACKGROUND

As mentioned earlier, the area of ESG is very wide and can be understood in different ways by different people. In this chapter, we will stick to some simple definitions. Firstly, there are many *ESG initiatives*, such as the Principles for Responsible Investment (PRI) (Principles for Responsible Investment, 2022), which provide a voluntary framework by which investors can incorporate ESG issues into their decision making and ownership practices so that they can align their objectives with those of society at large. The Circular Economy Action Plan is an example of an ESG initiative in Europe. The European Union also aims to introduce a new standard (European Council, 2019).

Secondly, the term *ESG goal* refers to any requirement associated with an ESG initiative. For example, PRI promotes principles such as "Principle 1: we will incorporate ESG issues into investment analysis and decision-making processes" which can be considered an ESG goal. Another example is the Circular Economy Action Plan that "encourages information sharing for continuous value re-co-creation between participants in a supply chain to reduce waste and enhance positive economic, environmental and social impacts". We can see that such ESG goals can be very general or prescriptive. Changes are frequent, and many goals have been evolving from general recommendations to mandatory obligations, so they are treated the same way in this report.

Thirdly, the concept of an *ESG stakeholder* refers to any organization pursuing or promoting ESG goals at a national level or global level. In this chapter, we are primarily interested in stakeholders with essential analytics requirements in pursuing an ESG goal. Table 3.1 shows examples of ESG initiatives, stakeholders and goals.

TABLE 3.1

Examples of ESG Initiatives, Stakeholders and Goals

Initiative	Goals	Important Stakeholders	References
International Financial Reporting Standard (IFRS)	Develop high-quality, understandable, enforceable and globally accepted accounting and sustainability disclosure standards	International Accounting Standards Board (IASB); International Sustainability Standards Board (ISSB)	(IFRS Foundation, 2023)
Investment Leadership Program (ILP)	Incorporating ESG factors into investment and ownership decisions	The United Nations, global policymakers and international network of investor signatories	(Principles for Responsible Investment, 2022)
UN Environment Program—Net-Zero Banking Alliance	Sets targets for climate protection and social progress	Banks in 41 countries	(The Alliance, 2021)
Prudential Practice Guide (CPG 229 Climate Change Financial Risks)	Outline prudent practices in relation to climate change financial risk management	APRA and Australian financial institutions	(Australian Prudential Regulation Authority, 2021)
GRI—Global Reporting 305 Emissions	Helps organizations be transparent and take responsibility for their impacts so that we can create a sustainable future	Used by more than 10,000 organizations in over 100 countries	(Global Sustainability Standards Board, 2018)
UN SDG (Sustainable Development Goals)	17 Sustainable Development Goals	All United Nations Members	(United Nations, 2023)
WELL and LEED certifications	Green Building Certification	Building owners and contracted consultants	(International WELL Building Institute, 2022; U.S. Green Building Council, 2021)
The National Greenhouse and Energy Reporting Act 2007 (NGER Act) in Australia	Inform government policy formulation and the Australian public; and Meet Australia's international reporting obligations	Local governments and financial institutions	(Australian Government, 2021)

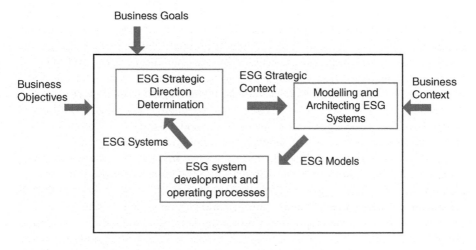

FIGURE 3.1   ESG research challenges.

3.3   ESG RESEARCH CHALLENGES

Developing new applications or extending existing infrastructures to efficiently address the new or emerging ESG requirements present many business and technical challenges that require further research studies.

Figure 3.1 shows three main interdependent research challenges from a stakeholder's point of view: strategizing, architecting and developing/operating ESG systems to respond to multiple forces (e.g. Business goals and objectives that include ESG, business context etc.).

3.3.1   ESG STRATEGIC DIRECTION DETERMINATION

The first challenge is evidently how organizations could transform through the incorporation of ESG goals into their existing strategies. There are currently no agreed-upon best practices to carry out this. A possible framework for integrating environmental, social and governance (ESG) considerations into an organization's strategy is first to conduct a materiality assessment (Sustainability Accounting Standards Board, 2023) to identify which ESG issues are most relevant and impactful for the organization. Next, the organization can set goals and targets related to the identified ESG issues and develop a plan to implement and track progress towards these goals (Global Sustainability Standards Board, 2023). Another important aspect of ESG stratification is to identify and manage risks and opportunities related to ESG issues (UN Global Compact, 2023). There is a need to evaluate the most effective framework towards the identification of a successful ESG strategy that will help to integrate ESG considerations into the organization's overall strategy and decision-making processes and to make sure that the organization is transparent about its approach and progress. The integration of ESG into organizational strategy is only the first of the challenges among others.

Mapping specific areas of businesses to specific environmental, social and governance (ESG) goals can be a complex and challenging task. Many businesses operate in multiple industries and have a wide range of products and services, making it difficult to identify which specific areas of the business are most relevant to ESG goals (Simnett & Huggins, 2015). Different businesses and industries may have different ESG concerns and priorities, which can make it challenging to map specific areas of the business to ESG goals as well as collect and standardize ESG data (Vitolla et al., 2019). In addition, the expanding scope of social and governance requires new risks and opportunities, such as AI and emerging technologies, to be integrated.

There is also a need to evaluate the most effective framework towards identifying a successful ESG strategy that will help integrate ESG considerations into the organization's overall strategy and decision-making processes and to make sure that the organization is transparent about its approach and progress. There is ongoing work in reference frameworks which provide a "common language" to facilitate discussions among ESG stakeholders and assist organizations in documenting and articulating their strategic context.

3.3.2 MODELLING AND ARCHITECTING ESG SYSTEMS

Creating new analytics models and architectures that leverage digital transformation technologies for ESG applications needs to be done at different levels of abstraction. The highest level is at the enterprise or the digital ecosystem architectural level. Organizations need to tailor their local enterprise architecture frameworks by combining elements from different frameworks that suit their specific needs (Vasauskaite & Gill, 2015). We need to research applying Enterprise architecture frameworks (Gill, 2015) or IoT reference frameworks (Nguyen, 2018) in the area of ESG. In addition, digital maturity models from an adaptive enterprise architecture perspective are needed (Alsufyani & Gill, 2021).

The next level of abstraction is the *technical architecture*. Operationalizing an analytics pipeline within an enterprise/corporate environment requires a high-quality analytics architecture that uses a combination of enabling technologies. There will be additional performance/security requirements that are not necessarily being addressed at the enterprise/digital ecosystem level. For this, it is important to have an architectural design approach that can satisfy multiple criteria (Yao et al., 2014): interoperability, integration, automation, reproducibility and efficient data handling.

An important challenge when modelling and architecting ESG systems is how to design an ESG data architecture, including monitoring, audit and assurance mechanisms to ensure that it is relevant, trustworthy and whether fit-for-purpose ("quality") data is being collected, used and re-used for supporting the ESG goals. ESG data sources are often from second and third parties in supply chains. A key consideration is the modelling and architecting for trust across data and software supply chains. There is a need for distributed trust in the supply chain and certificate technologies to be incorporated early. Increasingly, companies are also concerned about software supply chain integrity and AI risks within the organization and from their suppliers; integrating responsible AI risks with traditional ESG risks is another key research direction.

Many organizations need new quantitative models that would enable them to understand the direct contribution of their operations towards ESG goals or compliance with regulations. It is generally accepted that ESG data quality issues result in poor outcomes (e.g. when estimating carbon emissions); so, more sophisticated analysis techniques (e.g. AI/deep learning) are needed to provide better estimates in data-poor environments. Connecting different types of models at different levels of abstractions across the analytics pipeline is itself a challenge as it requires unique integration and analysis of organizations goals, digital technologies and resource management. The workflows associated with an ESG application need to interact with structured and unstructured data sources and conduct custom data processing and analysis.

The complexity of analytics pipelines (particularly those that use AI/ML) also raises many challenges related to ensuring data quality issues, managing provenance information needed for transparency as well as organizing metadata when combining data from multiple sources. There is an active stream of research in explainability (Tiddi & Schlobach, 2022), which will need to be considered when developing analytical models.

3.3.3 ESG SYSTEM DEVOPS PROCESSES

Application development and operating processes are needed once we understand the scope and degree of transformation required. In terms of methodologies, ESG presents the same challenges as IoT application development in which the following areas deserve further research (Fahmideh & Zowghi, 2020; Fahmideh et al., 2022):

- **A one-size-fits-all assumption is not a practical choice:** There is a need to investigate how to design situation-specific ESG-based systems that meet a specific project's functional and non-functional requirements.
- **Requirements analysis is missing:** An important issue in relation to the requirements analysis is the identification of key stakeholders because ESG projects are typically large at scale and involve a variety of stakeholder groups with different objectives, requirements and commitment levels. An area for future research is to extend existing approaches or to design ESG-specific requirement analysis techniques that pay attention to stakeholders' identification, prioritization and engagement.
- **Definition of roles not exploited:** Although the approaches define some roles attuned to ESG-based system development, their definitions and responsibilities are not adequately explicated. Such an approach has positive contributions to ESG development such as (i) making clear the responsibilities of each stakeholder in the course of an ESG system development and maintenance, (ii) defining the priority for responsibilities and (iii) specifying necessary interaction and cooperation between the roles.

For ESG frameworks to be an integral part of the organization, adopting rigorous software development approaches for building and maintaining cost-effective ESG applications that can evolve according to stakeholder is needed. Associated systems and IT infrastructure have to be designed with ESG goals in mind. Activities in the ESG data lifecycle such as data extraction and modelling need to be appropriately intertwined with software engineering tasks such as requirements engineering, design, verification and solution validation (Grabar et al., 2022).

When designing software applications, ESG should not be an afterthought. Relevant functional as well as non-functional requirements for ESG should be identified and incorporated in the system design stage whenever possible. Organizations lack tools and guidelines to implement ESG frameworks that integrate well with their organization's IT infrastructure and ESG goals. Ad hoc solutions often do not perform well, and are hard to maintain, when new requirements emerge over time. Even a slight shift in the organizational ESG framework such as adding a new metric or integrating a new data source may require complete re-engineering of the existing platforms and processes (Bandara & Rabhi, 2020).

New agile development processes adapted to the analytics pipeline's nature and how to develop/upgrade the IT infrastructure to implement the requirements and various other design decisions are needed. As the analysis in the data lifecycle tends to be very static and done in snapshots, there is a need for ongoing analysis and reporting at a finer scale. In addition, although ESG has led to the creation of networks of organizations that are aligned on shared goals, one challenge is how to effectively make these ecosystems efficiently collaborate, for example, in enabling ESG data and metrics sharing.

3.4   ESG DECISION-MAKING SYSTEMS

Since our focus is on supporting ESG goals from a quantitative perspective, this section discusses the data processing requirements in a typical ESG decision-making system and its associated challenges.

From a software system's perspective, business analytics solutions are often designed as a complex pipeline of transformations that operate across multiple layers, involving multiple technologies and systems. To facilitate the discussion in this chapter, we identify three layers which are the data collection, data processing and application layers. We discuss the requirements of each layer in the rest of this section.

3.4.1   DATA COLLECTION LAYER

Data collected at this layer is referred to as raw data. The ESG data comprise "E", "S" and "G", three pillars of data which include amounts of data, respectively. It can take different forms. For example, the "E" pillar data from the sensor, which is an important category for ESG data, includes indoor/outdoor air temperature and air quality data, water quality data, lighting data, motion/occupancy detecting data, light intensity data, electricity and natural gas consumption data. Other data types derive from "S" or "G" pillar data such as social indicators (e.g. employee well-being and mental health), financial variables (e.g. stock market data, macroeconomic data), news and social media data, corporate announcements, invoices etc.

The data collection layer involves accessing raw data from various real-time information-collecting devices (e.g. IoT devices), remote access to databases, Open data APIs etc. Many data sources will be from second and third parties so it is essential to establish a certain level of data provenance and trust.

3.4.2 DATA PROCESSING LAYER

Processed data comes in the form of various ESG metrics with various objective or subjective interpretations. It is a quantitative process of integrating ESG factors from different pillars. Metrics can be formula-based such as air quality metrics, greenhouse gas emissions and emission intensity or based on heuristic estimations such as environmental R&D and investment in renewable energy. These metrics are derived from the raw data using various data processing and analytics techniques such as time series data forecasting, machine learning, natural language processing etc. The data processing layer may itself be composed of many layers that constitute hierarchies of metrics at different granularity levels that can be amalgamated in the form of reports.

Several companies offer complete sets of ESG metrics and ratings. For example, Table 3.2 shows the popular and broadly accepted ESG score providers.

TABLE 3.2
Examples of ESG Rating Providers

ESG Ratings Provider	ESG Ratings Product	Coverage	References
Sustainalytics ESG	ESG Risk Score	20,000+ Companies	(Morningstar Sustainalytics, 2023a)
Sustainalytics-EU SFDR	ESG Risk Score	12,000+ Companies	(Morningstar Sustainalytics, 2023b)
Refinitiv ESG	ESG Score	12,000+ Companies	(Refinitiv, 2023)
MSCI	ESG Rating	14,000 Companies	(MSCI, 2023)
RepRisk	ESG Risks	210,000+ Companies	(RepRisk, 2023)
Bloomberg	Comprehensive set of ESG variables including Environmental (e.g. Air Quality) and Governance (e.g. Board Independence) metrics	14,000+ Companies	(Bloomberg, 2023)
ISS ESG Rating	ESG Fund Rating, ESG Rating & Rankings, Cyber Risk Score	11,900 Companies	(Institutional Shareholder Services, 2023)
S&P Global	ESG Credit Rating	8000 Companies	(S&P Global Ratings, 2023)
FTSE Russel	ESG Indices (e.g. Emerging Asia ESG Index and All-Share ESG Index)	7000 Companies	(FTSE Russell, 2023)

One limitation of these metric databases is that their ESG scoring is very basic and can be static (does not change frequently or reflect the latest state).

3.4.3 APPLICATION LAYER

There could be many different applications that use processed data in different ways. Each application can integrate a number of techniques for visualizing information and facilitating reporting and decision making via intuitive interfaces and dashboards. We identify different categories of users of data processing pipelines, such as:

- Listed corporations. To check whether they are satisfying ESG goals (e.g. understand the direct greenhouse gas emissions contribution of their operations to the environment)
- Investors, credit rating agencies (e.g. valuing companies) and investment firms
- Executives. Systems that can inform corporate strategic objectives (e.g. create carbon-efficiency supply chains)
- Associations/ESG professional agencies/consulting

Many corporations, particularly those involved in a tight value chain, desire a strong integration and connection with their partner's applications as quality and predictability gain importance. For example, a corporation that produces goods or services may need to know the suppliers of their suppliers and the customers of their customers. Therefore, the application layer can also be part of a digital ecosystem of ESG stakeholders rather than enclosed within a single enterprise. Some examples of applications are given in the next section.

3.4.4 EXAMPLE 1: AIR QUALITY MONITORING

In recent years, promoting health and well-being in the built environment has gained significant attention. The WELL Building Standard (International WELL Building Institute, 2022) is an international assessment tool that measures, certifies and monitors the performance of building features that impact health and well-being. Advancements in technology, such as the implementation of Internet of Things (IoT) devices, cloud-based databases and DevOps, and machine learning models, have provided new opportunities for monitoring, forecasting and reporting on the performance of buildings against the WELL standard. These technologies enable organizations to collect and process large amounts of data to gain insights into their buildings' health and well-being performance and comply with the standard. Additionally, the use of cloud-based databases and DevOps allows for more efficient data processing pipelines and machine learning models to be built and deployed to forecast and report on performance, which is essential for achieving compliance with the standard.

In this case study, we assume a company whose goal is to monitor their compliance with the WELL standard using AI and cloud technologies. Their existing certification process involves a manual process of inspection, which can be time-consuming and error-prone. Building a "custom" AI model to assist with this process has limitations;

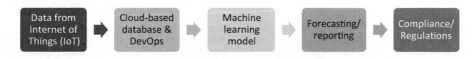

FIGURE 3.2 Example of an analytics pipeline for a certification process.

it is only valid at one point in time and can be costly to develop. An ideal solution would be to automate the continuous data gathering and processing with IoT devices and use AI techniques for checking compliance. This would allow for real-time monitoring and more accurate compliance checks, reducing the need for manual inspections and minimizing the potential for errors. By leveraging IoT, cloud systems and AI, organizations can improve their compliance with regulations and gain a more comprehensive understanding of their ESG performance.

The workflow for monitoring and verifying the quality of the built environment using IoT, cloud-based databases, DevOps, machine learning models, forecasting, reporting and compliance with regulations (shown in Figure 3.2) can be described as follows:

- IoT devices are deployed in a building to collect data on various environmental factors such as temperature, humidity and air quality.
- The data is transmitted to a cloud-based database for storage and processing.
- DevOps techniques are used to build and deploy machine learning models that can analyze the data and provide insights into the building's environmental performance.
- The models forecast future environmental conditions and generate reports on the building's compliance with international standards and regulations.
- The reports are used by the building management to identify areas where improvements can be made and to ensure compliance with regulations.

As the process is continuous, the data is collected and analyzed on a regular basis. The machine learning models are also regularly updated as needed to ensure accuracy, avoid model drift and adapt to new regulations.

3.4.5 EXAMPLE 2: CLIMATE CHANGE FINANCIAL RISK MANAGEMENT

There are increasing climate disclosure initiatives established by various boards such as the Task Force on Climate-related Financial Disclosure (TCFD) and Taskforce on Nature-related Financial Disclosure (TNFD), and new requirements arise from International Financial Reporting Standards (IFRS). Meanwhile, carbon pricing through emissions trading schemes (ETS) and carbon taxes/levies is gaining momentum globally. Those demand more accurate reporting to meet evolving global regulatory reporting requirements and implement improvements to abate emissions through an emission-efficient supply chain. Beyond reporting, there are also risk-management objectives relating to climate in the form of mitigating extreme weather conditions, especially in industries such as agriculture. Even financial institutions need to monitor

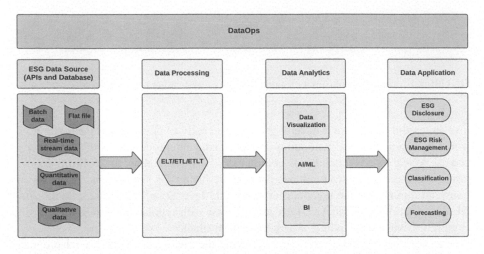

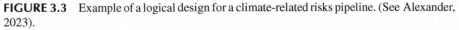

FIGURE 3.3   Example of a logical design for a climate-related risks pipeline. (See Alexander, 2023).

indirect (Scope 3) greenhouse gas emissions in their portfolio as part of international and national recommendations (GHG Protocol, 2013).

This case study is based on evidence that many organizations require a decision-making system that would enable them to quantify information, such as greenhouse gas emissions and climate-related risks and help them understand the direct contribution of their operations to the environment (Batulan et al., 2021). Such a system will have the following requirements (Figure 3.3):

- **Data collection layer:** Data is collected from qualitative and quantitative sources such as ESG events through different news flows and greenhouse gas emissions (can be direct or indirect (e.g. from the use of purchased energy).
- **Data processing layer:** Computes risk metrics associated with direct and indirect emissions and uses these (in combination with other more classic credit risk metrics) to compute core business metrics (e.g. credit risk, losses or investment returns).
- **Application layer:** Performing what-if scenarios, e.g. modelling the impact of climate events or the impact of adaptation measures.

(Board, 2017)

The DataOps pipelines (Alexander, 2023) start from collecting textual/qualitative/ unstructured and quantitative data via APIs or database connections. Then, the data processing and data analytics processes depend on functionality requirements. For example, supporting risk-management application measures the risk regarding different topic/metrics aligned with TCFD, TNFD or GHG protocol compliance. Such systems include quantitative and qualitative metric measurements. They will divide risk into financial material and non-financial metrics and then calculate the risk. Metrics comprise but are not limited to the following factors:

- **Quantitative factors:** GHG emission, emissions budgets, targets and trajectories and carbon prices;
- **Qualitative factors:** Direction of change or economic features, ESG events in news flow relevant to policy and legal risk, technology risk, market risk and reputation risk.

Other important functions in the system include:

- **Classification and Forecasting:** The classification function in the system can detect whether an event is risky. The forecasting function predicts the future event or carbon prices in the trade market.
- **Climate Disclosure:** The system supports firm ESG reports by its risk index, which can be used in TCFD, TNFD and other frameworks.

In this case study, the overall system serves to forecast firm sustainability risk and supply sights of their policy and compliance, which can assist firms and regulators in decision making and green fund investment. Besides, the firm can use this system to create and disclose its ESG report to relevant regulatory bodies.

3.5   CONCLUSIONS

This chapter has examined the area of ESG systems and outlined the research challenges and, in particular, in relation to building ESG decision-support systems. One major challenge that we outline is the inconsistent terminology and nomenclature that has been associated with ESG which makes it hard to have consistent meaning for ESG scores and metrics across multiple industries. ESG communities need to develop a better understanding of ESG concepts, models and data through the use of a common vocabulary.

Developing new ESG systems or extending existing infrastructures to efficiently address the new or emerging ESG requirements present many business and technical challenges that require further research studies. We identified three main interdependent research challenges from a stakeholder's point of view: strategizing, architecting and developing/operating ESG systems to respond to multiple forces. In the application section, our focus is on designing decision-making systems that support ESG goals from a quantitative perspective and outlining the data processing requirements in a typical ESG analytics solution and its associated challenges.

In conclusion, the area of ESG system development requires new reference architectures and processes to enable information and data processing services interoperability in the data analytics pipeline. New DevOps processes have to be designed accordingly. Incorporating a reference architecture that encourages requirement engineering and knowledge management in a way that will help organizations address the ESG challenges is discussed in this chapter.

ACKNOWLEDGMENTS

This chapter is based on an earlier report titled "Research Challenges and Future Directions in Supporting ESG Data Processing Applications" (unpublished). We wish to thank Asif Gill and Madhushi Bandara from the University of Technology Sydney, Mehdi Fahmideh from the University of Southern Queensland, Qinghua Lu and Liming Zhu from Data61 and Gavin Whyte from BrewAI for their contributions to this report.

REFERENCES

Alexander, P. (2023a, February 2). *What Data Pipeline Architecture should I use?* Google Cloud.

Alexander, P. (2023b). What Data Pipeline Architecture should I use?. Retrieved February 20, 2023, from https://cloud.google.com/blog/topics/developers-practitioners/what-data-pipeline-architecture-should-i-use

The Alliance. (2021, March 12). *UN-Convened Net-Zero Asset Owner Alliance.* https://www.unepfi.org/net-zero-alliance/

Alsufyani, N., & Gill, A. Q. (2021). A Review of Digital Maturity Models from Adaptive Enterprise Architecture Perspective: Digital by Design. *2021 IEEE 23rd Conference on Business Informatics (CBI), 01,* pp. 121–130. https://doi.org/10.1109/CBI52690.2021.00023

Australian Government. (2021). *The National Greenhouse and Energy Reporting Act 2007.* https://www.legislation.gov.au/Details/C2021C00509

Australian Prudential Regulation Authority. (2021). *Prudential Practice Guide: CPG 229 Climate Change Financial Risks.* https://www.apra.gov.au/consultation-on-draft-prudential-practice-guide-on-climate-change-financial-risks

Bandara, M., & Rabhi, F. A. (2020). Semantic Modeling for Engineering Data Analytics Solutions. *Semantic Web, 11,* 525–547. https://doi.org/10.3233/SW-190352

Batulan, C., Tan, F. T. C., & Chan, C. (2021, January). *Bridging the Sustainability Leadership Chasm: A Case Study of the Sustainability Advantage Program of the NSW Government, Australia.* https://doi.org/10.24251/HICSS.2021.579

Bloomberg. (2023). *Global Environmental, Social & Governance – ESG Data.* Retrieved January 26, 2023, from https://www.bloomberg.com/professional/dataset/global-environmental-social-governance-data/

Board, F. S. (2017). *The Use of Scenario Analysis in Disclosure of Climate-Related Risks and Opportunities.* https://www.tcfdhub.org/resource/tcfd-recommendations-technical-supplement-the-use-of-scenario-analysis-in-disclosure-of-climate-related-risks-and-opportunities/

European Council. (2019). *Sustainable Finance: Council Agrees Position on a Unified EU Classification System.* https://www.consilium.europa.eu/en/press/press-releases/2019/09/25/sustainable-finance-council-agrees-position-on-a-unified-eu-classification-system/

Fahmideh, M., & Zowghi, D. (2020). An Exploration of IoT Platform Development. *Information Systems, 87,* 101409. https://doi.org/10.1016/j.is.2019.06.005

Fahmideh, M., Ahmad, A., Behnaz, A., Grundy, J., & Susilo, W. (2022). Software Engineering for Internet of Things: The Practitioners' Perspective. *IEEE Transactions on Software Engineering, 48*(8), 2857–2878. https://doi.org/10.1109/TSE.2021.3070692

FTSE Russell. (2023). *FTSE ESG Index Series.* Retrieved January 26, 2023, from https://www.ftserussell.com/products/indices/esg

GHG Protocol. (2013). Technical Guidance for Calculating Scope 3 Emissions. *Supplement to the Corporate Value Chain (Scope 3), Accounting & Reporting Standard, in Partnership with the Carbon Trust.*

Gill, A. (2015). *Adaptive Cloud Enterprise Architecture.* World Scientific Publishing Co. Pte. Ltd.

Global Sustainability Standards Board. (2018). *GRI 305: Emissions 2016.* https://www.globalreporting.org/standards/media/1012/gri-305-emissions-2016.pdf

Global Sustainability Standards Board. (2023). *GRI Standards.* Retrieved January 26, 2023, from https://www.globalreporting.org/standards

Grabar, N., Tsu, L. & Grannis, H. (2022). *SEC's Climate Disclosure Rules: GHG Emissions* Disclosure Requirements. Retrieved January 26, 2023, from https://corpgov.law.harvard.edu/2022/05/06/secs-climate-disclosure-rules-ghg-emissions-disclosure-requirements/

International Financial Reporting Standards. (2023).IFRS Foundation. Retrieved January 26, 2023, from https://www.ifrs.org/about-us/who-we-are/

Institutional Shareholder Services. (2023). *ISS ESG Rating.* Retrieved January 26, 2023, from https://www.issgovernance.com/esg/

International WELL Building Institute. (2022). *WELL Performance Rating.* https://v2.wellcertified.com/en/performance-rating/overview

Morningstar Sustainalytics. (2023a). *Company ESG Risk Ratings.* Retrieved January 26, 2023, from https://www.sustainalytics.com/esg-ratings

Morningstar Sustainalytics. (2023b). *EU Sustainable Finance Action Plan Solutions.* Retrieved January 26, 2023, from https://www.sustainalytics.com/landing-pages/sustainable-finance-disclosure-regulation-solutions

MSCI. (2023). *ESG Ratings.* Retrieved January 26, 2023, from https://www.msci.com/our-solutions/esg-investing/esg-ratings

Nguyen, N. & Tett, M. (2018). *IoT Reference Framework.* Retrieved January 26, 2023, from https://www.iot.org.au/wp/wp-content/uploads/2016/12/IoT-Reference-Framework-v1.0.pdf

Principles for Responsible Investment. (2022, December 21). *Principles for Responsible Investment.* https://www.unpri.org/

Refinitiv. (2023). *Refinitiv ESG Company Scores.* Retrieved January 26, 2023, from https://www.refinitiv.com/en/sustainable-finance/esg-scores

RepRisk. (2023). *ESG Risks.* Retrieved January 26, 2023, from https://www.reprisk.com/

S&P Global Ratings. (2023). *ESG In Credit Ratings.* Retrieved January 26, 2023, from https://www.spglobal.com/ratings/en/research-insights/esg/esg

Simnett, R., & Huggins, A. L. (2015). Integrated reporting and assurance: where can research add value?. *Sustainability Accounting, Management and Policy Journal, 6*(1), 29–53.

Sustainability Accounting Standards Board. (2023). *SASB Standards: Materiality Map.* Retrieved January 26, 2023, from https://www.sasb.org/standards/

Tiddi, I., & Schlobach, S. (2022). Knowledge Graphs as Tools for Explainable Machine Learning: A Survey. *Artificial Intelligence, 302,* 103627.

U.S. Green Building Council. (2021). *LEED v4.1 Operation and Maintenance Beta Guide.* https://www.usgbc.org/resources/leed-v41-om-beta-guide

UN Global Compact. (2023). *UN Global Compact.* Retrieved January 26, 2023, from https://www.unglobalcompact.org/

United Nations. (2023). *17 Sustainable Development Goals.* Retrieved January 25, 2023, from https://sdgs.un.org/goals

Vasauskaite, J., & Gill, A. (2015). Rethinking Enterprise Architecture for Sustainable Energy System Development. *Journal of Electronic Science and Technology, 13*(3), 212–220. https://doi.org/10.11989/JEST.1674-862X.505151

Vitolla, F., Raimo, N., & Rubino, M. (2019). Appreciations, criticisms, determinants, and effects of integrated reporting: A systematic literature review. *Corporate Social Responsibility and Environmental Management, 26*(2), 518–528.

Yao, L., Rabhi, F., & Peat, M. (2014). *Supporting Data-Intensive Analysis Processes: A Review of Enabling Technologies and Trends* (Vol. 2, pp. 481–508). https://doi.org/10.4018/978-1-4666-6178-3.ch019

4 Analysing Trust, Security and Cost of Cloud Consumer's Reviews using RNN, LSTM, and GRU

Muhammad Raheel Raza
Firat University, Elazığ, Turkey

Walayat Hussain and Mehdi Rajaeian
Peter Faber Business School, Australian Catholic University, Australia

4.1 INTRODUCTION

People frequently seek out the advice of others and ask for recommendations before making decisions. They share their suggestions online, thanks to public social media. Customers often search for a product before purchasing it, and online reviews have a major impact on their decision. Companies may learn more about people's thoughts and preferences by soliciting feedback on their goods through formal and informal communication channels [1]. In many cases, assessing sentiments independently for each business factor is more valuable than obtaining the general sentiment of a topic.

Sentiment analysis is analyzing online conversations and discussions such as Twitter tweets, blog posts, or comments about certain services or subjects and categorizing the users' perspectives (positive, negative, and neutral) to determine consumer sentiment regarding items [2]. Sentiment Analysis is a computer research or approach for programmatically separating thoughts from metadata. It enables organizations to get a true sense of their customer's feelings about their products and handle massive volumes of data in a timely and cost-effective way. Brands can listen closely to their consumers and customize goods and services to fit their requirements by automatically evaluating client input, from survey replies to social media chats [3]. One of the types of sentiment classification involves Aspect-based Sentiment Analysis (ABSA). ABSA also known as Entity/Feature-based Sentiment Analysis is a method for evaluating customer evaluations and projecting an overall impression on any item or brand utilized in a variety of sectors. ABSA detects the features of a

DOI: 10.1201/9781003340621-4

product evaluation and determines which class of emotion each component belongs to. However, ABSA faces several challenges including the co-extraction of aspects or entities (opinion targets) from a corpus, as well as the identification and modelling of the relationships between them.

Artificial intelligence (AI) is a collection of algorithms and knowledge that attempts to replicate human intellect. One of these is machine learning, and deep learning is among the machine learning approaches. Deep learning is an AI function that attempts to replicate the ability of the human brain to analyze data and recognize patterns to make choices. Deep learning is an artificial intelligence subclass of machine learning that employs networks smart enough to learn from unstructured or unidentified data in an unsupervised way [4]. Deep Learning is a subfield of AI that is focused on computer algorithms learning and making predictions on their own. Deep learning employs artificial neural networks that are meant to mimic how people think and learn as opposed to traditional machine learning algorithms, which use simpler rules and mathematical models [5]. It employs algorithms to mimic the functioning of neurons in the human brain. Deep learning develops artificial neural networks and layers that are modelled after the human brain. It's a machine learning approach that instructs computers to perform human-related tasks naturally and easily, learning from patterns encountered. Artificial neural networks power deep learning with multiple layers. Deep Neural Networks (DNNs) are networks with several layers that can execute sophisticated operations like representation and abstraction to understand visual, audio and textual data. Image categorization, language translation, and speech recognition have all benefited from deep learning. It can handle any pattern recognition issue without the need for human interaction. Some of the deep learning methods include Deep feedforward neural network (D-FFNN), Convolutional Neural Network (CNN), Recurrent Neural Network (RNN), Long Short-term Memory (LSTM) and Gated Recurrent Unit (GRU).

Cloud Computing is one of the most significant computing paradigms in Information Technology. The distributed software architecture gave rise to the cloud computing idea. The goal of cloud computing is to deliver hosted services through the internet. Cloud computing has led to the emergence of new user groups and industries in recent decades. Its services are provided through data centers located across the globe. Some of the popular cloud services include Microsoft Office 365 and Google Apps [6]. Cloud Computing is a model for providing convenient, on-demand network access to computing assets such as programs, servers, storage systems, application frameworks, and communication systems, and they are housed at a remote data center managed by service providers [7]. A Service Level Agreement (SLA) is a contract between a cloud service provider and a client that guarantees a certain level of performance [8, 9]. In any event, if a service provider fails to fulfil the set minimums, the provider is obligated to pay the agreed-upon penalty to the cloud service customer. As more clients use Service Oriented Architecture (SOA), the quality and dependability of the services become more essential [10]. Service users have unique needs that vary significantly. To reach a compromise, negotiation is necessary. This is where SLA comes in and establishes the baseline for the expected level of service that the provider can provide. Our research work focuses on the ABSA process upon CSCs' feedback about different CSPs on the basis of three basic attributes: Security, Trust, and Cost.

This chapter is structured as follows. In Section 4.2, a brief literature review of ABSA in deep learning within the cloud paradigm is provided. Section 4.3 explains the deep learning approaches utilized for sentiment classification tasks. The implementation is discussed in Section 4.4, and the results of the analysis performed are provided in Section 4.5. Finally, Section 4.6 concludes this chapter.

4.2   RELATED WORKS

4.2.1   ASPECT-BASED SENTIMENT CLASSIFICATION

This section presents a review of literature on aspect-based sentiment analysis using deep learning approaches.

Al-Ghuribi et al. [11] proposed an approach to tackle the challenges of aspect-based sentiment analysis in large-scale unlabeled datasets in the real world. Their method combines frequency-based (word level) and syntactic-relation-based (phrase level) approaches. It also incorporates a semantic similarity-based technique to extract domain-relevant aspects, even when they are not frequently mentioned in the reviews. An overall sentiment score is calculated after determining the weight of aspects and their ratings in the phrases. Alqarayouti et al. [12] performed aspect-based sentiment analysis on government-based smart applications. The study intends to assist government agencies in gaining a better understanding of their customers' requirements and expectations. To achieve this, a hybrid approach to sentiment analysis that combines domain lexicons and rules classifying the app reviews was proposed [13]. The proposed approach aimed to extract key aspects from reviews and categorize the resulting sentiments. The proposed approach uses Natural Language Processing (NLP) strategies, rules, and lexicons to generate a summary of the findings. Kok et al. [14] emphasized on the review-level position of aspect-based sentiment analysis. They forecast the sentiment of a specific element in a study. A two-stage sentiment analysis method is proposed for this purpose. Domain ontology is used to forecast sentiment in the first step. If the domain ontology is uncertain, a backup step based on an SVM bag-of-words model is used. In addition, word embeddings are employed to enhance the coverage of domain ontology by discovering semantically similar terms.

Karimi et al. [15] analyzed the language used in reviews by employing deep learning models. They used a combination of modules, namely BERP and parallel aggregation for aspect extraction tasks and Hierarchal aggregation to carry out aspect sentiment classification activities. Deep learning methods outperform traditional methods in achieving maximum model performance for such a challenging task. Mohammadi and Shaverizade [16] integrated the benefits of several deep learning models by presenting a unique technique for aspect-based sentiment analysis that employs deep ensemble learning. Four deep learning models, such as CNN, LSTM, BiLSTM, and GRU are used in the suggested technique. The outputs of these models are then merged using a stacking ensemble method, with logistic regression serving as the meta-learner. Raza et al. [17] compared different research articles focusing on the sentiment classification of cloud reviews. Most of the articles utilized machine learning approaches, while deep learning techniques resulted in higher accuracy.

The various datasets used and the domain of classifications are also determined. Shams et al. [18] designed a LISA (language independent sentiment analysis) method comprising three stages. The English and Persian datasets are evaluated to extract previous domain knowledge that results in selecting preliminary polarity lexicon and aspect word sets. As basic information, these two resources are fed into an expectation–maximization algorithm, which determines the likelihood of every word based on its aspect and mood. The final stage involves the evaluation of the document and classifying each aspect with respect to its polarity.

To achieve a finer-grained analysis, Zainuddin et al. [19] considered the usage of an aspect-based sentiment classification on Twitter. By using a feature-selection approach, they presented a novel hybrid sentiment categorization for Twitter. The study compared the classification accuracy of three different feature-selection approaches, namely principal component analysis (PCA), latent semantic analysis (LSA), and random projection (RP) feature selection. The proposed approach was evaluated on Twitter datasets from various domains, and the results revealed that it provided significant findings when compared to various classification algorithms. Zhang et al. [20] address the problems in other sentiment analysis approaches by introducing a weakly supervised classifier of a deep-level semi-autonomous sentiment annotation system based on the bidirectional encoder representation from transformers (BERT). Problems like insufficiency and inaccuracy of data are solved by annotating the restaurant reviews under 18 aspects. Using this annotated data, they provide a unique classification model for particular features, based on standard machine learning algorithms and annotation systems, to investigate consumer preferences, genuine consumer sentiments, and repurchase intent. The suggested method can improve the ABSA task accuracy while reducing space–time complexities. Zhao et al. [21] performed aspect-based sentiment analysis using a combination of convolutional neural network (CNN) and gated recurrent unit (GRU) deep learning models. CNN's generated local features, and the long-term dependency mechanism of GRU achieved excellent aspect extraction results, resulting in better sentiment classification of aspects within hotel and car datasets used for evaluation.

4.2.2 CLOUD COMPUTING SERVICE SELECTION

The study [22] conducts a comparative examination of several time-series prediction methodologies utilizing machine learning methods. These methods seek to control SLA violations by establishing feasible service level agreements (SLAs) in the cloud. By using the right methodologies and anticipating future Quality of Service (QoS) characteristics based on the conditions, cloud service providers may reduce the risk of service violations and fines. The results showed the accuracy of several time–series machine-learning prediction algorithms. In SMEs, authors [23] have tested several QoS prediction algorithms for resource management and risk mitigation against SLA violations. All of the methodologies, including neural network techniques, stochastic methods, and time–series methods, were tested across various time intervals and projected resource usage in the post-interaction time phase when SLA is set up and implemented. The ARIMA technique had the greatest forecast accuracy results among all methods.

The Centralized Cloud Service Repository (CCSR) [24] architecture aids cloud service customers in selecting acceptable cloud services and quickly finding relevant services for them. The Harvesting-as-a-Service (HaaS) module of the framework assists in harvesting online data without scripting and arranging it in various ways. The service repository component locates various cloud services and serves as a source of available cloud services for service consumers to use. In addition, the system gives real cloud reviews dataset for cloud services. From the standpoint of the service consumer, the article [25] highlights one of the most important factors in identifying SLA violations. A cloud service consumer's previous resource consumption profile can forecast the likelihood of service violations in the cloud. It predicts future possibilities for similar circumstances, prompting the service provider to take action. Furthermore, the profile history of nearby customers can be used for this purpose.

The need to maintain confidence in cloud computing has been stressed by the authors [26]. Trust is a key factor in forming a sustainable SLA and a trustworthy service provider–consumer relationship. Continuous SLA monitoring is one of the ways to maintain confidence. The self-manageable case-based reasoning method, the SLA-based trust model approach, the broker-based approach and the reputation-based and process composition approach are all presented. In order to determine the features of the methods, a comparison study is also carried out.

4.3   DEEP LEARNING APPROACHES

4.3.1   RECURRENT NEURAL NETWORK (RNN)

Recurrent Neural Networks (RNNs) are a type of feedforward neural network. RNNs function on the premise of storing a layer's output and feeding it back into the input for anticipating the layer's outcome. It may conduct the same job or operation on a series of inputs repeatedly [27, 28]. An RNN contains an internal memory that allows it to recall or recall information from the input it receives, which aids in the system's context acquisition. As a result, a RNN is an excellent fit for processing sequential-type data, such as time series data. A CNN or feedforward neural network can't achieve this because it can't figure out the relationship between prior and subsequent inputs.

To express the internal working within a cell in an RNN structure, let us consider the input, hidden, and output layers to be represented by "int", "hid", and "out", respectively. For the current state of a cell occurring at a time "t", an amalgam of two inputs, "inp_t" and "hid_{t-1}" are fed into the cell and the equation forms as:

$$hid_t = f\left(hid_{t-1}, inp_t\right)$$

After applying the tanh activation function and individual weights of input and hidden states to the equation of the current hidden state, we get:

$$hid_t = \tan_h\left(W_{hid}{}^* hid_{t-1} + W_{inp}{}^* inp_t\right)$$

As a result, the output from the output layer "$out_{(t)}$" will be as follows:

$$out_t = W_{out}{}^* hid_t$$

Here, $W_{(out)}$ is the weight of output and $hid_{(t)}$ is the current hidden state.

4.3.2 Long Short-Term Memory (LSTM)

The RNN model should be trained for backpropagation purposes. Backpropagation requires complex calculations of weight gradients to achieve each time step interconnected with each other. During this process, long sequences of data within a cell require high computational cost and adequate operational time [27, 28]. This results in gradient vanishing and exploding gradient problems. As a solution to such complications, LSTM proves to be the best option.

Long Short-Term Memory (LSTM) is a class of RNNs that can learn long-term dependencies, which is useful for solving sequence prediction issues. LSTM contains feedback connections, which means it can process the full sequence of data. This is useful in speech recognition, machine translation, and other areas. The LSTM is a kind of RNN that performs exceptionally well on a wide range of gradient-related issues by remembering past information. Three types of gates operate on the information flow into and out of the cell of LSTM for data processing, the input, forget, and output gates. Each new entry of data is performed through the input gate of the cell. The forget gate ignores the unnecessary data and removes it from the cell. The output gate provides the output achieved from the cell.

For the forget gate "for" at time "t", an input "inp" and previous hidden state "hid" are passed to the sigmoid activation function to determine the amount of data to forget.

$$for_t = \sigma \left[W_{for}{}^* \left(hid_{t-1}, inp_t \right) + bias_{for} \right]$$

The amount of data to be saved within the memory cell is decided by two equations. Firstly, the above combination is passed through the sigmoid activation function. Secondly, the activation function is now replaced by tan_h with the same inputs.

$$input = \sigma \left[W_{input}{}^* \left(hid_{t-1}, inp_{ut} \right) + bias_{input} \right]$$

$$cand'_t = \tanh \left[W_{cand'}{}^* \left(hid_{t-1}, inp_{ut} \right) + bias_{cand'} \right]$$

The previous cell state "cand(t-1)" is updated by using formula:

$$cand_t = \left(cand_{t-1}{}^* for_t \right) + \left(input_t{}^* cand'_t \right)$$

For the output gate, the equations are as follows:

$$out_t = \sigma \left[W_{out}{}^* \left(hid_{t-1}, inp_{ut} \right) + bias_{out} \right]$$

$$hid_t = out_t{}^* cand_t$$

This gives the value of the current hidden state, which is a product of two entities.

4.3.3 GATED RECURRENT UNIT (GRU)

Gated Recurrent Unit (GRU) is a type of RNNs, similar to LSTM but has two operational gates, the reset and update gates replacing the output gate in LSTM. These gates aid in handling the vanishing gradient problem within the memory cell. Using less memory and faster than LSTM, GRU maintains a hidden state instead of a cell state as in LSTM [27, 28]. The reset gate is responsible for maintaining a hidden state as follows:

$$res_t = \sigma \left[W_{res}{}^* \left(hid_{t-1}, inp_t \right) \right]$$

The update gate handles the long-term memory of the cell as follows:

$$upd_t = \sigma \left[W_{upd}{}^* \left(hid_{t-1}, inp_t \right) \right]$$

The hidden state "hid" is determined by first calculating a candidate's hidden state, as:

$$hid'_t = \tanh \left[W_{hid}{}^* \left[\left(hid_{t-1}, res_t \right) + inp_t \right] \right]$$

The candidate hidden state is then used to achieve the current hidden state value:

$$hid_t = \left(upd_t{}^* hid_{t-1} \right) + \left(1 - upd_t \right)^* hid'_t$$

4.4 EXPERIMENTATION

This section explains the implementation performed for sentiment classification using the mentioned deep learning approaches. The main headings include the description of CCF dataset, configuration of hyper-parameters that includes the no of epochs, activation function selection, optimizer selection, dropout value, and learning rate etc. A brief description of the aspects identified and their sentiment score per review calculated are also mentioned.

4.4.1 DATASET

The dataset used in our study is the Cloud Consumer Feedback (CCF) dataset. It comprises a set of textual reviews by various service consumers related to their experiences while attaining diverse cloud services from different service providers. The service feedback points are extracted through the Harvesting-as-a-Service (HaaS) method by mining disparate web portals. The dataset contains all the information regarding the reviews, review title, reviewer, date of review posting, review rating, and service information etc. There are a total of 10,000 consumer feedbacks rated with numbers from 1 to 5. Based on ratings, the reviews are categorized into positive, negative, and neutral reviews. Nine thousand three hundred fifty reviews are indicated to be positive, 421 reviews as negative, while the rest 222 are considered to be neutral-natured reviews. The division of the training and testing sample of the dataset is 80:20. Table 4.1 is an overview of the division of reviews in the CCF dataset.

4.4.2 ASPECT EXTRACTION

In our performed study, Aspect-based Sentiment Analysis (ABSA) is used to extract various aspects from the cloud consumer feedback dataset. All the service feedback is analyzed based on three aspect categories: Security, Trust, and Cost. The polarities of individual reviews for each mentioned aspect are calculated using RNN, LSTM, and GRU. Table 4.2 shows the division of training and testing reviews as per the aspects and their classification of sentiments.

TABLE 4.1
Division of Training and Testing Samples in the CCF Dataset

CCF	Training Sample	Validation Sample	Testing Sample	Total
Total reviews	7820	223	1957	10,000
Percentage	78.207%	2.23%	19.57%	100%

TABLE 4.2
Classification of CCF According to Aspects and Their Sentiments

Aspects	Training	Testing	No. of Reviews		
			Positive	Negative	Neutral
Security	188	47	86	8	2
Trust	19	5	16	7	1
Cost	334	84	379	29	10

4.4.3 HYPER-PARAMETERS CONFIGURATION

The model employed is sequential in nature, with layers stacked in a linear fashion. Each model has a single layer that corresponds to the layer name. Using the spatial dropout layer with a dropout value of 0.1, the overfitting problem is averted. For all three models, a learning rate of 0.001 balances learning ability and the Sigmoid activation function. Table 4.3 shows the model's different hyper-parameters for the neural network architecture.

4.5 RESULTS

The outcomes of the performed experiments are listed in this section. RNN, LSTM, and GRU deep learning methods are used to train the algorithm using a training dataset. Each classifier in our study goes through up to 50 epochs of training. The model trains automatically through the whole training dataset in one cycle inside one epoch. The test sample is then tested on the algorithm based on the findings received after the training step. To determine the accuracy rates of the defined models per epoch, Tables 4.4, 4.5, and 4.6 give an overview of how deep learning models process with respect to each aspect. The evaluations show that the RNN model performs better than the LSTM and GRU approaches.

Table 4.7 highlights the performance results for each aspect category. It shows that the Trust category achieves the highest accuracy while the least value appears for the Cost aspect category.

Using the aspects identified, various cloud services offered by different cloud providers are prioritized based on the sentiment polarity scores, which are calculated by analyzing individual reviews. A short description of some service providers with their polarity scores w.r.t aspects is given in Table 4.8. It is evident from the table that Nutcache achieved the highest sentiment score in terms of Trust, while Rerun is the most secure service provider based on the score value. However, Vision Helpdesk is a cost-friendly provider to different service consumers.

TABLE 4.3

Overview of Hyper-parameters Configuration

Hyper-parameters	CCF Dataset
Model	Sequential
Epochs	10
Hidden Layer	3
Activation Function	Sigmoid
Optimizer	Adam
Dropout Value	0.1
Learning Rate	0.001
Batch Size	32

TABLE 4.4
Performance Evaluation of Deep Learning Methods for Trust Aspect

Epochs	LSTM	GURU	RNN
1st	0.4211	0.3158	0.1579
2nd	0.6842	0.7368	0.4374
3rd	0.6842	0.6842	0.7368
4th	0.7368	0.6842	0.8421
5th	0.7368	0.6842	0.8421
6th	0.6842	0.6842	0.7895
7th	0.6842	0.6842	0.8421
8th	0.6842	0.7368	0.8421
9th	0.6842	0.7368	0.7895
10th	0.6842	0.7368	0.8421

TABLE 4.5
Performance Evaluation of Deep Learning Methods for Security Aspect

Epochs	LSTM	GURU	RNN
1st	0.7368	0.5132	0.5526
2nd	0.8816	0.8816	0.8816
3rd	0.8816	0.8816	0.8816
4th	0.8816	0.8816	0.8816
5th	0.8816	0.8816	0.8816
6th	0.8816	0.8816	0.8816
7th	0.8816	0.8816	0.8947
8th	0.8816	0.8816	0.8816
9th	0.8816	0.8816	0.9211
10th	0.8816	0.8816	0.9211

TABLE 4.6
Performance Evaluation of Deep Learning Methods for Cost Aspect

Epochs	LSTM	GURU	RNN
1st	0.8563	0.8413	0.8413
2nd	0.9102	0.9102	0.9102
3rd	0.9102	0.9102	0.9102
4th	0.9102	0.9102	0.9102
5th	0.9102	0.9102	0.9102
6th	0.9102	0.9102	0.9192
7th	0.9102	0.9222	0.9222
8th	0.9102	0.9341	0.9491
9th	0.9341	0.9551	0.9701
10th	0.9341	0.9641	0.9731

TABLE 4.7

Division of Training and Testing Samples in the CCF Dataset

Aspects	Precision (%)	Recall (%)	F1 Score (%)	Accuracy (%)
Security	95.00	98.00	96.00	95.00
Trust	85.00	94.00	92.00	85.00
Cost	89.00	97.00	93.00	89.00

TABLE 4.8

Cloud Providers w.r.t Aspects and Their Polarity Scores

Cloud Providers	Category	Aspect	Polarity Scores
Incapsula	Customer Service & Support	Security	0.45522
Spiratest	IT Management	Cost	0.12940
Nutcache	Project Management	Trust	0.90520
Capsule CRM	Customer Management	Security	0.40611
Vision Helpdesk	Customer Service & Support	Cost	0.61974
Leankit	Operations Management	Trust	0.51060
Apptivo CRM	Customer Management	Cost	0.36632
Rerun	Finance & Accounting	Security	0.68080
Cats	HR & Employee Management	Trust	0.51060

To express the accuracy rates achieved by the deep learning approaches per epoch graphically, a graphical representation is given for each aspect (see Figure 4.1).

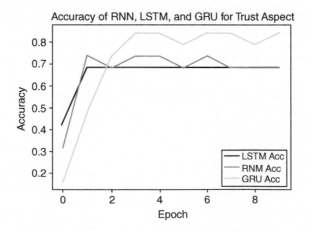

FIGURE 4.1 Graphical representations of accuracy rates achieved by RNN, LSTM, and GRU for given aspects.

(Continued)

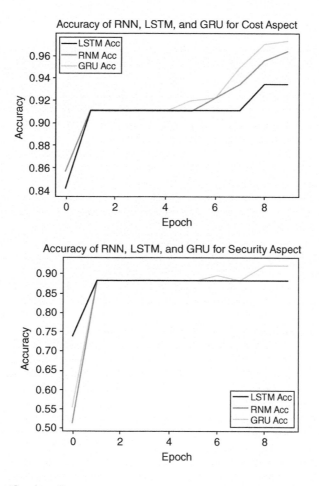

FIGURE 4.1   (Continued)

4.6   CONCLUSION

Deep learning methods demonstrated great efficacy in performing sentiment analysis tasks efficiently with high precision and accuracy. In this study, aspect-based sentiment analysis is performed using deep learning approaches including RNN, LSTM, and GRU to extract aspects from cloud dataset reviews and classify them into positive, negative, or neutral categories. It also prioritizes the cloud services offered by cloud service providers based on the aspects extracted from the reviews and calculates the polarity of aspects within the reviews. Among the deep learning methods, RNN outperformed LSTM and GRU in accuracy rates and performance for sentiment classification of cloud consumer feedback. Overall, this study demonstrates the potential of deep learning methods for performing aspect-based sentiment analysis and extracting valuable insights from customer feedback.

REFERENCES

[1] M. R. Raza, W. Hussain, and A. Varol, "Performance analysis of deep approaches on Airbnb sentiment reviews," in *2022 10th International Symposium on Digital Forensics and Security (ISDFS)*, 2022, pp. 1–5: IEEE.

[2] A. Alghamdi, W. Hussain, A. Alharthi, and A. B. Almusheqah, "The need of an optimal QoS repository and assessment framework in forming a trusted relationship in cloud: A systematic review," in *2017 IEEE 14th International Conference on e-Business Engineering (ICEBE)*, 2017, pp. 301–306: IEEE.

[3] B. A. Alrashed and W. Hussain, "Managing SLA Violation in the cloud using Fuzzy re-SchdNeg Decision model," in *2020 15th IEEE Conference on Industrial Electronics and Applications (ICIEA)*, 2020, pp. 136–141: IEEE.

[4] H. Butt, M. R. Raza, M. J. Ramzan, M. J. Ali, and M. Haris, "Attention-based CNN-RNN Arabic Text Recognition from Natural Scene Images," *Forecasting*, vol. 3, no. 3, pp. 520–540, 2021.

[5] W. Hussain, J. M. Merigó, M. R. Raza, and H. Gao, "A new QoS prediction model using hybrid IOWA-ANFIS with fuzzy C-means, subtractive clustering and grid partitioning," *Information Sciences*, vol. 584, pp. 280–300, 2022.

[6] M. R. Raza and A. Varol, "QoS parameters for viable SLA in cloud," in *2020 8th International Symposium on Digital Forensics and Security (ISDFS)*, 2020, pp. 1–5: IEEE.

[7] W. Hussain, M. R. Raza, M. A. Jan, J. M. Merigo, and H. Gao, "Cloud risk management with OWA-LSTM predictive intelligence and fuzzy linguistic decision making," *IEEE Transactions on Fuzzy Systems*, vol. 30, no. 11, pp. 4657–4666, 2022.

[8] M. R. Raza and A. Varol, "Digital Currency Price Analysis Via Deep Forecasting Approaches for Business Risk Mitigation," in *2021 2nd International Informatics and Software Engineering Conference (IISEC)*, 2021, pp. 1–5: IEEE.

[9] W. Hussain and J. M. Merigo, "Onsite/offsite social commerce adoption for SMEs using fuzzy linguistic decision making in complex framework," *Journal of Ambient Intelligence and Humanized Computing*, vol. 14, pp. 1–20, 2022.

[10] A. M. Alkalbani and W. Hussain, "Cloud service discovery method: A framework for automatic derivation of cloud marketplace and cloud intelligence to assist consumers in finding cloud services," *International Journal of Communication Systems*, vol. 34, no. 8, p. e4780, 2021.

[11] S. M. Al-Ghuribi, S. A. M. Noah, and S. Tiun, "Unsupervised semantic approach of aspect-based sentiment analysis for large-scale user reviews," *IEEE Access*, vol. 8, pp. 218592–218613, 2020.

[12] O. Alqaryouti, N. Siyam, A. A. Monem, and K. Shaalan, "Aspect-based sentiment analysis using smart government review data," *Applied Computing Informatics*, vol. 19, 2020.

[13] M. R. Raza and S. Alkhamees, "Deep learning analysis of Australian stock market price prediction for intelligent service oriented architecture," in *IoT as a Service: 7th EAI International Conference, IoTaaS 2021, Sydney, Australia, December 13–14, 2021, Proceedings*, 2022, pp. 173–184: Springer.

[14] S. De Kok and F. Frasincar, "Using word embeddings for ontology-driven aspect-based sentiment analysis," in *Proceedings of the 35th Annual ACM Symposium on Applied Computing*, 2020, pp. 834–842.

[15] A. Karimi, L. Rossi, and A. Prati, "Improving BERT Performance for Aspect-Based Sentiment Analysis," 2020.

[16] A. Mohammadi and A. Shaverizade, "Ensemble deep learning for aspect-based sentiment analysis," *International Journal of Nonlinear Analysis Applications*, vol. 12, pp. 29–38, 2021.

[17] M. R. Raza, W. Hussain, E. Tanyıldızı, and A. Varol, "Sentiment analysis using deep learning in cloud," in *2021 9th International Symposium on Digital Forensics and Security (ISDFS)*, 2021, pp. 1–5: IEEE.

[18] M. Shams, N. Khoshavi, and A. Baraani-Dastjerdi, "LISA: Language-independent method for aspect-based sentiment analysis," *IEEE Access*, vol. 8, pp. 31034–31044, 2020.

[19] N. Zainuddin, A. Selamat, and R. Ibrahim, "Hybrid sentiment classification on twitter aspect-based sentiment analysis," *Applied Intelligence*, vol. 48, no. 5, pp. 1218–1232, 2018.

[20] Y. Zhang, J. Du, X. Ma, H. Wen, and G. Fortino, "Aspect-based Sentiment Analysis for User Reviews," *Cognitive Computation*, pp. 1–14, vol. 13, 2021.

[21] N. Zhao, H. Gao, X. Wen, and H. Li, "Combination of convolutional neural network and gated recurrent unit for aspect-based sentiment analysis," *IEEE Access*, vol. 9, pp. 15561–15569, 2021.

[22] W. Hussain, J. M. Merigo, and M. R. Raza, "Predictive intelligence using ANFIS-induced OWAWA for complex stock market prediction," *International Journal of Intelligent Systems*, vol. 37, no. 8, pp. 4586–4611, 2022.

[23] A. Tahira, W. Hussain, and A. Ali, "Based Recommender System for Hedonic and Utilitarian products in IoT Framework," in *IoT as a Service: 7th EAI International Conference, IoTaaS 2021, Sydney, Australia, December 13–14, 2021, Proceedings*, 2022, pp. 221–232: Springer.

[24] A. M. Alkalbani, W. Hussain, and J. Y. Kim, "A centralised cloud services repository (CCSR) framework for optimal cloud service advertisement discovery from heterogenous web portals," *IEEE Access*, vol. 7, pp. 128213–128223, 2019.

[25] W. Hussain, J. M. Merigo, H. Gao, A. M. Alkalbani, and F. A. Rabhi, "Integrated AHP-IOWA, POWA framework for ideal cloud provider selection and optimum resource management," *IEEE Transactions on Services Computing*, vol. 16, no. 1, pp. 370–382, 2021.

[26] W. Hussain, H. Gao, M. R. Raza, F. A. Rabhi, and J. M. Merigo, "Assessing cloud QoS predictions using OWA in neural network methods," *Neural Computing Applications*, vol. 34, pp. 1–18, 2022.

[27] M. R. Raza, W. Hussain, and J. M. Merigó, "Long short-term memory-based sentiment classification of cloud dataset," in *2021 Innovations in Intelligent Systems and Applications Conference (ASYU)*, 2021, pp. 1–6: IEEE.

[28] M. R. Raza, W. Hussain, and J. M. Merigó, "Cloud sentiment accuracy comparison using RNN, LSTM and GRU," in *2021 Innovations in Intelligent Systems and Applications Conference (ASYU)*, 2021, pp. 1–5: IEEE.

5 Interval Type-2 Fuzzy Decision Analysis Framework Based on Online Textual Reviews

Xiao-Hong Pan and Shi-Fan He
Fuzhou University, Fujian, China
University of Jaén, Jaén, Spain

Diego García-Zamora and Luis Martínez
University of Jaén, Jaén, Spain

5.1 INTRODUCTION

According to the "wisdom of the crowd" theory, the decisions made by a large group of nonexpert decision-makers may be smarter than those made by a small group of experts [1, 2]. Although gathering such a large group of decision-makers could have been a complex task some years ago due to mobility costs or lack of space [3, 4], the development of social networks provides a huge source of nonexpert opinions about almost any topic [5, 6] that could be considered to make intelligent decisions [4]. Nevertheless, the data that can be found on the Web lacks a common structure [7]. In particular, the most usual format of unstructured information is the text expressed in natural language, but how to exploit the information contained in textual reviews to make decisions is still an open problem.

In this regard, one of the main challenges to be addressed is related to the management of the uncertainties derived from either vagueness (fuzziness) or incompleteness (ignorance) [8, 9]. A widely used classical representation scheme in decision making used to model the uncertainties inherent to incompleteness is the Linguistic Distribution Assessments (LDA) introduced by Zhang et al. [10, 11]. On the other hand, the management of uncertainties related to vagueness has been traditionally addressed with the fuzzy linguistic approach. In particular, the interval type-2 fuzzy sets (IT2FSs) proposed by Mendel et al. [12] are considered an effective tool for computing with words.

Therefore, this proposal introduces a multi-criteria decision analysis framework for Online Textual Reviews (OTRs) that models both imprecision and incompleteness by hybridizing IT2FSs and LDAs. First, we introduce a processing mechanism to transform unstructured online reviews into a distributed assessment framework. Then, an entropy-based interval type-2 fuzzy weights determination model is

DOI: 10.1201/9781003340621-5

developed to capture the uncertainty of the criteria. Afterward, the Evidential Reasoning (ER) approach [13] is extended to aggregate the interval type-2 distributed information. Moreover, some rules are provided to generate the expected utility of each alternative. Finally, a minimax regret approach is defined to rank interval-valued expected utilities that improves existing interval-valued ranking approaches.

The remaining sections are summarized as follows. In Section 5.2, the basic notions necessary to understand the proposal are reviewed. Section 5.3 presents our multi-criteria decision-making framework for managing OTRs based on IT2FSs and LDAs. Section 5.4 shows the performance of our proposal when solving a multi-criteria decision problem. Finally, Section 5.5 highlights some conclusions.

5.2 PRELIMINARIES

To make the study self-contained, this section introduces some basic concepts about IT2FSs, the entropy-based weight determination model, the evidential reasoning approach, and the minimax regret approach.

5.2.1 INTERVAL TYPE-2 FUZZY SETS

The concept of IT2FSs was initially proposed by Mendel et al. [14, 15] on the basis of the type-2 fuzzy sets defined by Zadeh [16]. To date, the IT2FSs have been widely applied to deal with the uncertainty involved in decision-making processes [17–21]. Some basic theories and methods about IT2FSs are introduced below.

Definition 1

(T2FS [14, 15]). Suppose that $\mu_{\tilde{A}}(x,u)$ is the type-2 fuzzy membership function of type-2 fuzzy set (T2FS) $\tilde{A}$ and the T2FS $\tilde{A}$ can be expressed as:

$$\tilde{A} = \left\{ \left((x,u), \mu_{\tilde{A}}(x,u) \right) \mid \forall x \in X, \forall u \in J_x \in [0,1] \right\}$$

where X is the universe of discourse of $\tilde{A}$, u is primary membership at $x \in X$, representing the belief degree of x belonging to A, and $\mu_{\tilde{A}}(x,u)$ denotes the membership of primary membership, that is, secondary membership. Moreover, the T2FS also can be denoted as follows:

$$\tilde{A} = \int_{x \in X} \int_{u \in J_x} \mu_{\tilde{A}}(x,u) / (x,u)$$

Definition 2

(IT2FS [14, 15]). If all the values of the secondary membership are equal to 1, that is, $\mu_{\tilde{A}}(x,u) = 1$, then $\tilde{A}$ is called IT2FS and can be expressed by the following mathematical formula:

$$\tilde{A} = \int_{x \in X} \int_{u \in J_x} 1/(x, u)$$

In which, x is the main variable and $J_x \in [0, 1]$ represents the primary membership at x.

It should be highlighted that different membership functions will lead to different interval type-2 fuzzy formats. In this regard, the trapezoidal IT2FSs proposed by Chen and Chang [22] is one of the most widely used IT2FSs in decision making.

Definition 3

(Trapezoidal [22]). The trapezoidal IT2FS defined in the universe of discourse X can be expressed in the following form:

$$\tilde{A} = \left(\mu_{\tilde{A}}^L, \mu_{\tilde{A}}^U \right) = \left[\left(a_1^L, a_2^L, a_3^L, a_4^L, h^L\left(\tilde{A}\right) \right), \left(a_1^U, a_2^U, a_3^U, a_4^U, h^U\left(\tilde{A}\right) \right) \right]$$

where a_1^L, a_2^L, a_3^L, a_4^L, a_1^U, a_2^U, a_3^U, and a_4^U are crisp values and satisfy $0 \le a_1^L \le a_2^L \le a_3^L \le a_4^L$, $0 \le a_1^U \le a_2^U \le a_3^U \le a_4^U$, $a_1^U \le a_1^L$ and $a_4^L \le a_4^U$; $h^L\left(\tilde{A}\right)$ and $h^U\left(\tilde{A}\right)$ denote the heights of trapezoidal IT2FS, satisfying $0 \le h^L\left(\tilde{A}\right) \le h^U\left(\tilde{A}\right) \le 1$. The membership functions of the trapezoidal IT2FS are defined in the following way (see Fig 5.1).

$$\mu_{\tilde{A}}^L(x) = \begin{cases} \dfrac{h^L\left(\tilde{A}\right) \cdot \left(x - a_1^L\right)}{a_2^L - a_1^L}, & a_1^L \le x < a_2^L \\[3mm] h^L\left(\tilde{A}\right), & a_2^L \le x < a_3^L \\[3mm] \dfrac{h^L\left(\tilde{A}\right) \cdot \left(a_4^L - x\right)}{a_4^L - a_3^L}, & a_3^L \le x < a_4^L \\[3mm] 0, & \text{otherwise} \end{cases}$$

$$\mu_{\tilde{A}}^U(x) = \begin{cases} \dfrac{h^U\left(\tilde{A}\right) \cdot \left(x - a_1^U\right)}{a_2^U - a_1^U}, & a_1^U \le x < a_2^U \\[3mm] h^U\left(\tilde{A}\right), & a_2^U \le x < a_3^U \\[3mm] \dfrac{h^U\left(\tilde{A}\right) \cdot \left(a_4^U - x\right)}{a_4^U - a_3^U}, & a_3^U \le x < a_4^U \\[3mm] 0, & \text{otherwise} \end{cases}$$

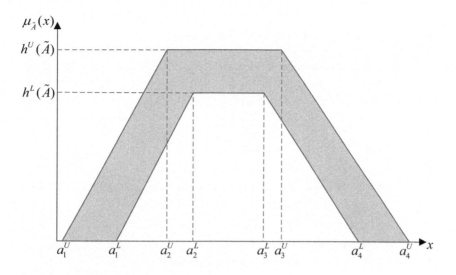

FIGURE 5.1 The interval type-2 fuzzy sets.

Definition 4

[23, 24] Suppose that $\tilde{A} = \left[\left(a_1^l, a_2^l, a_3^l, a_4^l, h^L\left(\tilde{A}\right)\right), \left(a_1^U, a_2^U, a_3^U, a_4^U, h^U\left(\tilde{A}\right)\right)\right]$ and $\tilde{B} = \left[\left(b_1^l, b_2^l, b_3^l, b_4^l, h^L\left(\tilde{B}\right)\right), \left(b_1^U, b_2^U, b_3^U, b_4^U, h^U\left(\tilde{B}\right)\right)\right]$ be two trapezoidal IT2FSs, then the arithmetic operations between $\tilde{A}$ and $\tilde{B}$ are defined as:

$$\tilde{A} + \tilde{B} = \begin{bmatrix} \left(a_1^l + b_1^l, a_2^l + b_2^l, a_3^l + b_3^l, a_4^l + b_4^l, \min\left\{h^L\left(\tilde{A}\right), h^L\left(\tilde{B}\right)\right\}\right), \\ \left(a_1^U + b_1^U, a_2^U + b_2^U, a_3^U + b_3^U, a_4^U + b_4^U, \min\left\{h^U\left(\tilde{A}\right), h^U\left(\tilde{B}\right)\right\}\right) \end{bmatrix}$$

$$\tilde{A} \cdot \tilde{B} = \begin{bmatrix} \left(a_1^l \cdot b_1^l, a_2^l \cdot b_2^l, a_3^l \cdot b_3^l, a_4^l \cdot b_4^l, \min\left\{h^L\left(\tilde{A}\right), h^L\left(\tilde{B}\right)\right\}\right), \\ \left(a_1^U \cdot b_1^U, a_2^U \cdot b_2^U, a_3^U \cdot b_3^U, a_4^U \cdot b_4^U, \min\left\{h^U\left(\tilde{A}\right), h^U\left(\tilde{B}\right)\right\}\right) \end{bmatrix}$$

$$\lambda \cdot \tilde{A} = \left[\left(\lambda a_1^l, \lambda a_2^l, \lambda a_3^l, \lambda a_4^l, h^L\left(\tilde{A}\right), \left(\lambda a_1^U, \lambda a_2^U, \lambda a_3^U, \lambda a_4^U, h^U\left(\tilde{A}\right)\right)\right)\right], \lambda \geq 0$$

$$\tilde{A}^q = \left[\left(\left(a_1^l\right)^q, \left(a_2^l\right)^q, \left(a_3^l\right)^q, \left(a_4^l\right)^q, h^L\left(\tilde{A}\right)\right), \left(\left(a_1^U\right)^q, \left(a_2^U\right)^q, \left(a_3^U\right)^q, \left(a_4^U\right)^q, h^U\left(\tilde{A}\right)\right)\right], q \geq 0$$

5.2.2 ENTROPY-BASED WEIGHT DETERMINATION MODEL

The concept of entropy is derived from thermodynamics and it is a useful tool to measure the information contained in the data from an objective perspective [25]. Recently, entropy has also been applied to determine the criteria weights in multi-criteria decision-making problems [25–28]. The entropy-based weight deter-mination model mainly consists of the following stages:

Stage 1: **Calculate the entropy of criterion C_j.** If the evaluation value of the alternative Z_i with respect to the criterion C_j is given by the crisp value $\tilde{r}_{ij}$, then the entropy of criterion C_j can be calculated by:

$$E_j = -\frac{1}{\log n} \sum_{i=1}^{m} \hat{r}_{ij} \log \hat{r}_{ij}, j = 1, 2, \ldots, n.$$

where n represents the number of criteria, m is the number of alterna-tives, and $\hat{r}_{ij} := \dfrac{r_{ij}}{\sum_{i=1}^{m} r_{ij}}$.

Stage 2: **Calculate the dispersion of criterion C_j.** After obtaining the entropy, the dispersion of criterion C_j can be computed by:

$$\xi_j = 1 - E_j, j = 1, \ldots, n.$$

Stage 3: **Calculate the criteria weights.** Based on the dispersion of criterion C_j, we can obtain the weight of criterion C_j by the following equation:

$$w_j = \frac{\xi_j}{\sum_{j=1}^{n} \xi_j}, j = 1, \ldots, n.$$

5.2.3 EVIDENTIAL REASONING ALGORITHM

The ER algorithm [29], which was developed on the basis of the Dempster–Shafer theory of evidence [30], is an effective tool for dealing with MCDM problems under uncertainty. This algorithm mainly consists of three stages: constructing the basic probability masses, fusing the basic probability masses under multiple criteria, and generating the expected utilities of alternatives.

The basic probability assignments (BPAs) are the basic information units in Dempster–Shafer theory of evidence:

Definition 5

(BPA [13]). Let $H = \{H_1, \ldots, H_N\}$ be a collectively exhaustive and mutually exclu-sive set of hypotheses or propositions, which is also called the frame of discern-ment. A BPA is a function $m : 2^\theta \to [0, 1]$ satisfying the following conditions:

$$m(\varnothing) = 0,$$
$$\sum_{A \subseteq \theta} m(A) = 1,$$

where $\varnothing$ denotes the empty set and 2^Θ stands for the power set of the frame of discernment:

$$2^\Theta = \left\{ \varnothing, \{H_1\}, \ldots, \{H_N\}, \{H_1, H_2\}, \ldots, \{H_1, H_N\}, \{H_1, \ldots, H_{N-1}\}, \Theta \right\}$$

Suppose that there are m alternatives $Z_1, \ldots, Z_m$, the basic probability assignments of Z_i under C_j supporting H_k can be generated by:

$$m_{k,j}(Z_i) = w_j \cdot \beta_{k,j}(Z_i), k = 1, \ldots, N, j = 1, \ldots, n$$

$$m_{H,j}(Z_i) = 1 - \sum_{k=1}^{N} m_{k,j}(Z_i) = 1 - w_j \cdot \sum_{k=1}^{N} \beta_{k,j}(Z_i), j = 1, \ldots, n$$

$$\bar{m}_{H,j}(Z_i) = 1 - w_j, j = 1, \ldots, n$$

$$\tilde{m}_{H,j}(Z_i) = w_j \cdot \left(1 - \sum_{k=1}^{n} \beta_{k,j}(Z_i) \right), j = 1, \ldots, n$$

where $\beta_{k,j}(Z_i)$ denotes the belief degree of alternative Z_i under criterion C_j belonging to grade H_k, which satisfies $\beta_{k,j}(Z_i) \geq 0$ and $\sum_{k=1}^{N} \beta_{k,j}(Z_i) \leq 1$; w_j is the weight of criterion C_j and satisfies $w_j \geq 0$ and $\sum_{j=1}^{n} w_j = 1$.

These BPAs are usually aggregated according to the analytical ER algorithm [13]:

$$m_k(Z_i) = \rho \cdot \left[\prod_{j=1}^{n} \left(m_{k,j}(Z_i) + \bar{m}_{H,j}(Z_i) + \tilde{m}_{H,j}(Z_i) \right) - \prod_{j=1}^{n} \left(\bar{m}_{H,j}(Z_i) + \tilde{m}_{H,j}(Z_i) \right) \right], k = 1, \ldots, N$$

$$\tilde{m}_H(Z_i) = \rho \cdot \left[\prod_{j=1}^{n} \left(\bar{m}_{H,j}(Z_i) + \tilde{m}_{H,j}(Z_i) \right) - \prod_{j=1}^{n} \tilde{m}_{H,j}(Z_i) \right], k = 1, \ldots, N$$

$$\bar{m}_H(Z_i) = \rho \cdot \left[\prod_{j=1}^{n} \bar{m}_{H,j}(Z_i) \right]$$

$$\rho = \left[\sum_{k=1}^{N} \prod_{j=1}^{n} \left(m_{k,j}(Z_i) + \bar{m}_{H,j}(Z_i) + \tilde{m}_{H,j}(Z_i) \right) - (N-1) \prod_{j=1}^{n} \left(\bar{m}_{H,j}(Z_i) + \tilde{m}_{H,j}(Z_i) \right) \right]^{-1}$$

$$\beta_k(Z_i) = \frac{m_k(Z_i)}{1 - \bar{m}_H(Z_i)}$$

$$\beta_H(Z_i) = \frac{\tilde{m}_H(Z_i)}{1 - \bar{m}_H(Z_i)}$$

where $\beta_k(Z_i)$ represents the belief degree of alternative Z_i belonging to H_k and $\beta_H(Z_i)$ is the unassigned belief degree.

Finally, the expected utilities of each alternative are generated according to the following equation.

$$u(Z_i) = \sum_{k=1}^{N} u(H_k) \cdot \beta_k(Z_i), i = 1, \ldots, m,$$

where $u(H_k)$ represents the utility of grade H_k.

If there is an unassigned belief degree, the expected utilities of alternatives are expressed by the interval values generated by [13]:

$$u^-(Z_i) = \sum_{k=1}^{N} \beta_k(Z_i) \cdot u(H_k) + \beta_H(Z_i) \cdot u(H_1), i = 1, \ldots, m$$

$$u^+(Z_i) = \sum_{k=1}^{N} \beta_k(Z_i) \cdot u(H_k) + \beta_H(Z_i) \cdot u(H_N), i = 1, \ldots, m$$

where $u^-(Z_i)$ and $u^+(Z_i)$ denote the lower and upper bounds of the expected utilities, respectively.

If there is no unassigned belief degree, that is, $\beta_H(Z_i) = 0$, then the expected utilities of alternatives are expressed by crisp values, that is, $u(Z_i) = u^-(Z_i) = u^+(Z_i)$.

5.2.4   MINIMAX REGRET APPROACH

Due to the fact that the intervals cannot be directly compared and ranked, several interval-valued ranking approaches have been proposed such as the possibility-based ranking approach [31], the average-based ranking approach [32], the dominance degree-based ranking approach [33], and the fuzzy preference relationship-based ranking approach [34]. However, these approaches fail to distinguish the interval values with the same center but different widths. For this reason, Wang et al. [35] proposed a minimax regret approach to compare and rank interval values. The specific comparison process is provided below.

Definition 6

(Maximum regret degree [35]). Let $u(Z_i) = [u(Z_i)^-, u(Z_i)^+]$, $i = 1, \ldots, m$ be m interval-valued expected utilities. Then, the maximum regret degree of $u(Z_k)$ is defined as:

$$MR(u(Z_k)) = \max\left\{\max_{i \neq k}\left\{u(Z_i)^+\right\} - u(Z_k)^-, 0\right\}$$

In this regard, the interval-valued expected utility with the minimum maximum regret degree (i.e., minimax regret degree) will be selected as the optimal one. The complete ranking process of interval-valued expected utilities can be generated by the following elimination steps.

Step 1: Calculate the maximum regret degree of each interval-valued expected utility. The interval-valued expected utility with the minimum maximum regret degree is selected as the optimal one. Suppose that $u(Z_{k1})$ is determined as the optimal interval-valued expected utility, where $1 \leq k_1 \leq m$.

Step 2: Eliminate the interval-valued expected utility $u(Z_{k1})$ from further consideration and recalculate the maximum regret degrees of the rest interval-valued expected utilities. Suppose that $u(Z_{k2})$ has the minimum maximum regret degree, then $u(Z_{k2})$ is determined as the optimal interval-valued expected utility, where $1 \leq k_1 \neq k_2 \leq m$.

Step 3: Eliminate the interval-valued expected utility $u(Z_{k2})$ from further consideration and recalculate the maximum regret degrees of the remaining interval-valued expected utilities. Suppose that the interval-valued expected utility $u(Z_{k3})$ is selected as the optimal one, where $1 \leq k_1 \neq k_2 \neq k_3 \leq m$.

Step 4: Repeat the above eliminating process until only one interval-valued expected utility $u(Z_{km})$ is left; then, the complete ranking order of all interval-valued expected utilities are $u(Z_{k1}) > u(Z_{k2}) > \ldots > u(Z_{km})$, where ">" denotes "is superior to."

5.3   AN ONLINE REVIEW-BASED INTERVAL TYPE-2 FUZZY DECISION-MAKING METHOD

This section proposes an OTR-based interval type-2 fuzzy decision-making method. First, a new information processing mechanism is developed to translate OTRs into an interval type-2 fuzzy distributed structure. Second, an entropy-based interval type-2 fuzzy weight determination model is proposed to compute the criteria weights. Then, the ER algorithm is extended to fuse the interval type-2 fuzzy distributed information. Finally, an improved minimax regret approach is applied to compare and rank the alternatives.

5.3.1   DISTRIBUTED STRUCTURE-BASED ONLINE REVIEW PROCESSING MECHANISM

OTRs contain a lot of useful information related to users and products that may play a vital role in decision making [36]. The OTRs provided by people are usually characterized by unstructured text information and, consequently, distributed structures are a potential tool to tackle such unstructured text information [37]. Hence, this section proposes a new OTR-processing mechanism by combing the IT2FSs and distributed structure.

Suppose that N_i online reviews related to alternative Z_i are collected through the crawler tool based on a Scrappy framework. First, after a preliminary analysis, several aspects are selected as the decision criteria, which are denoted as $C_1, \ldots, C_n$. With the aid of sentiment analysis, the emotional grading of the online reviews under each criterion is then obtained. The number of online reviews under criterion C_j belonging to positive grading is $\text{Num} - \text{Pos}(C_j)$, the number of online reviews belonging to negative grading is Num $-$ Neg(C_j) and the number of online reviews belonging to neutral grading is Num $-$ Neu(C_j). Afterward, the belief degree of alternative Z_i under criterion C_j belonging to the positive grading can be generated by:

$$\beta_{i,j}^{pos}(Z_i) = \frac{\text{Num} - \text{Pos}(C_j)}{N_i}$$

Similarly, the belief degree of alternative Z_i under criterion C_j belonging to the neutral grading and negative grading can be generated by:

$$\beta_{i,j}^{neu}(Z_i) = \frac{\text{Num} - \text{Neu}(C_j)}{N_i}$$

$$\beta_{i,j}^{neg}(Z_i) = \frac{\text{Num} - \text{Neg}(C_j)}{N_i}$$

As mentioned in Ref.[37], the outcomes of sentiment analysis include not only positive, negative, and neutral sentiments, but also ignorant sentiment. The belief degree of alternative Z_i under criterion C_j belonging to the ignorant grading can be calculated by:

$$\beta_{i,j}^{ign}(Z_i) = 1 - \beta_{i,j}^{pos}(Z_i) - \beta_{i,j}^{neu}(Z_i) - \beta_{i,j}^{neg}(Z_i)$$

The ignorant sentiment can be either positive, neutral, or negative [37]. When the ignorant sentiment is completely assigned to negative or neutral grading, the belief degree of alternative Z_i under criterion C_j belonging to the positive grading is still $\beta_{i,j}^{pos}(Z_i)$; when the ignorant sentiment is completely assigned to positive grading, the belief degree of alternative Z_i under criterion C_j belonging to the positive grading will be $\beta_{i,j}^{pos}(Z_i) + \beta_{i,j}^{ign}(Z_i)$. Hence, the belief degree of alternative Z_i under criterion C_j belonging to the positive grading can be characterized by the interval $\left[\beta_{i,j}^{pos}(Z_i), \beta_{i,j}^{pos}(Z_i) + \beta_{i,j}^{ign}(Z_i)\right]$. In the same way, the belief degrees of alternative Z_i under criterion C_j belonging to the negative grading and neutral grading is $\left[\beta_{i,j}^{neg}(Z_i), \beta_{i,j}^{neg}(Z_i) + \beta_{i,j}^{ign}(Z_i)\right]$ and $\left[\beta_{i,j}^{neu}(Z_i), \beta_{i,j}^{neu}(Z_i) + \beta_{i,j}^{ign}(Z_i)\right]$, respectively.

Through the proposed OTR-processing mechanism, the online reviews related to alternative Z_i can be transformed into distributed structure information with interval-valued belief degrees, that is, $H(Z_i) = \left\{ \text{Pos}, \left[\beta_{i,j}^{pos}(Z_i), \beta_{i,j}^{pos}(Z_i) + \beta_{i,j}^{ign}(Z_i)\right] \right.$; Neu, $\left[\beta_{i,j}^{neu}(Z_i), \beta_{i,j}^{neu}(Z_i) + \beta_{i,j}^{ign}(Z_i)\right]$; Neg, $\left. \left[\beta_{i,j}^{neg}(Z_i), \beta_{i,j}^{neg}(Z_i) + \beta_{i,j}^{ign}(Z_i)\right] \right\}, j = 1,$ ..., n. In which, Pos, Neu, and Neg are the abbreviations of the linguistic terms Positive, Neutral, and Negative. This distributed structure follows a Computing With Words (CWW) scheme in which the interval data driven-based CWW model [38] may be employed to perform the computations.

5.3.2 AN ENTROPY-BASED INTERVAL TYPE-2 FUZZY WEIGHTS DETERMINATION MODEL

In MCDM, distinct criteria usually have diverse effects on the decision results [39]. So far, many studies have focused on determining the weights of the criteria from different points of view [40–45]. However, most existing studies express the weights of the criteria using crisp values, which may fail to reflect the uncertainty of the criteria. To address this limitation, this subsection proposes an entropy-based interval type-2 fuzzy distributed weights determination model.

Suppose that there is an MCDM problem that consists of m alternatives and each alternative is influenced by n criteria. For the sake of simplicity, the alternatives and criteria are respectively denoted as $Z = \{Z_1, \ldots, Z_m\}$ and $C = \{C_1, \ldots, C_n\}$. The evaluation value of alternative Z_i with respect to criterion C_j is given by r_{ij}, where $\tilde{r}_{ij}$ is expressed by distributed information $H_{ij} = \left\{ \left(S_{k,ij}, \left[\beta_{k,ij}^-(Z_i), \beta_{k,ij}^+(Z_i) \right] \right) \mid k = 1, \ldots, K \right\}$. While, $S_{1,ij}$, $S_{2,ij}$, and $S_{3,ij}$ are the linguistic terms representing positive grading, neutral grading, and negative grading, $\left[\beta_{k,ij}^-(Z_i), \beta_{k,ij}^+(Z_i) \right]$ is the interval-valued belief degree corresponding to the linguistic terms. The distributed information can be obtained by the aforementioned OTR-processing mechanism. The weights of the criteria are represented by the vector $w = (w_1, \ldots, w_n)$ and can be generated by the following processes:

1. **Calculate the entropy of criterion C_j.** The entropy of criterion C_j can be obtained by solving the following pair of nonlinear programming models:

$$\max/\min E_j = -\frac{1}{\ln n} \times \sum_{i=1}^{m} f_{ij} \times \ln f_{ij}$$

$$s.t. \begin{cases} f_{ij} = \dfrac{\text{Score}(H_{ij})}{\sum\limits_{i=1}^{m} \text{Score}(H_{ij})}, & i = 1, \cdots, m, j = 1, \cdots, n \\[2ex] \text{Score}(H_{ij})^- \leq \text{Score}(H_{ij}) \leq \text{Score}(H_{ij})^+, & i = 1, \cdots, m, j = 1, \cdots, n \\[1ex] \text{Score}(H_{lj})^- \leq \text{Score}(H_{lj}) \leq \text{Score}(H_{lj})^+, & l = 1, \cdots, m, j = 1, \cdots, n \end{cases}$$

where Score(H_{ij}) is the score value of distributed information H_{ij} and can be calculated by:

$$\text{Score}(H_{ij}) = \left[\text{Cen}(S_k)^-, \text{Cen}(S_k)^+ \right] \cdot \left[\beta_{k,ij}^-(Z_i), \beta_{k,ij}^+(Z_i) \right]$$

$$= \left[\text{Cen}(S_k)^- \cdot \beta_{k,ij}^-(Z_i), \text{Cen}(S_k)^+ \cdot \beta_{k,ij}^+(Z_i) \right]$$

where H_{ij} denotes the distributed information of alternative Z_i with respect to criterion C_j; Cen(S_k)$^-$ and Cen(S_k)$^+$ represent the lower and upper bounds of the centroid of the IT2FS corresponding to linguistic term S_k.

Suppose that E_j^- and E_j^+ be the optimal solutions of the above pair of non-linear programming models, then the entropy of criterion C_j can be denoted by the interval $\left[E_j^-, E_j^+ \right]$.

2. **Calculate the dispersion of criterion C_j.** After obtaining the entropy of criterion C_j, the dispersion of criterion C_j can be accordingly determined. Because the entropy is expressed by interval value, the dispersion should also be interval value and its lower and upper bounds can be calculated by:

$$\xi_j^- = 1 - E_j^+$$
$$\xi_j^+ = 1 - E_j^-$$

3. **Determine the weight of criterion C_j.** Based on the dispersion of criterion C_j, the weight of criterion C_j can be determined by:

$$w_j = \left[w_j^-, w_j^+ \right] = \left[\frac{\xi_j^-}{\sum_{j=1}^{n} \xi_j^+}, \min\left\{ \frac{\xi_j^+}{\sum_{j=1}^{n} \xi_j^-}, 1 \right\} \right]$$

From the above analysis, we can observe that the criteria weights generated by the proposed weight determination model are characterized by interval values instead of crisp values.

5.3.3 AN EVIDENTIAL REASONING-BASED INFORMATION FUSION APPROACH

Evidential reasoning algorithm is a potentially effective tool to fuse the distributed information [13]. Thus, this subsection develops an evidential reasoning-based information fusion approach to fuse the interval type-2 fuzzy distributed information. The proposed approach mainly consists of three stages: construct the basic probability masses, fuse the basic probability masses, and generate the expected utilities of alternatives.

(1) **Transform the distributed information into basic probability masses**
    After obtaining the belief degrees and criteria weights, the distributed information can be transformed into basic probability masses. In this chapter, both the belief degrees and criteria weights are expressed by interval values, so the basic probability masses are also characterized by interval values and can be calculated by:

$$m_{k,j}(Z_i) = \left[w_j^- \cdot \beta_{k,j}^-(Z_i), w_j^+ \cdot \beta_{k,j}^+(Z_i) \right] \tag{5.1}$$

$$\bar{m}_{\Theta,j}(Z_i) = \left[1 - w_j^+, 1 - w_j^- \right] \tag{5.2}$$

$$\tilde{m}_{\Theta,j}(Z_i) = \left[w_j^- \cdot \beta_{\Theta,j}^-(Z_i), w_j^+ \cdot \beta_{\Theta,j}^+(Z_i) \right] \tag{5.3}$$

$$\beta_{\Theta,j}^{-}(Z_i) = \max\left(0, 1 - \sum_{k=1}^{N} \beta_{k,j}^{+}(Z_i)\right) \tag{5.4}$$

$$\beta_{\Theta,j}^{+}(Z_i) = 1 - \sum_{k=1}^{N} \beta_{k,j}^{-}(Z_i) \tag{5.5}$$

In which, $\beta_{k,j}(Z_i)$ represents the belief degree of the evaluation value $\tilde{r}_{ij}$ belonging to grade H_k, $\bar{m}_j(\Theta)$ is the ignorance caused by criteria weights and $\tilde{m}_j(\Theta)$ denotes the ignorance caused by the uncertainty of evaluation value. Moreover, the basic probability masses should satisfy the following condition:

$$\sum_{k=1}^{N} m_{k,j}(Z_i) + \bar{m}_{\Theta,j}(Z_i) + \tilde{m}_{\Theta,j}(Z_i) = 1$$

(2) **Fuse the basic probability masses under multiple criteria**
   After transforming the distributed information into basic probability masses, the fused interval-valued belief degree of each alternative can be calculated by solving the following pair of nonlinear programming models:

$$\text{max/ min } \beta_k(Z_i) = \frac{m_k(Z_i)}{1 - \bar{m}_{\Theta}(Z_i)}$$

$$\text{s.t.} \begin{cases} m_k(Z_i) = \rho \cdot \left[\prod_{j=1}^{n}\left(m_{k,j}(Z_i) + \bar{m}_{\Theta,j}(Z_i) + \tilde{m}_{\Theta,j}(Z_i)\right) - \prod_{j=1}^{n}\left(\bar{m}_{\Theta,j}(Z_i) + \tilde{m}_{\Theta,j}(Z_i)\right)\right] \\[2ex] \tilde{m}_{\Theta}(Z_i) = \rho \cdot \left[\prod_{j=1}^{n}\left(\bar{m}_{\Theta,j}(Z_i) + \tilde{m}_{\Theta,j}(Z_i)\right) - \prod_{j=1}^{n}\bar{m}_{\Theta,j}(Z_i)\right] \\[2ex] \bar{m}_{\Theta}(Z_i) = \rho \cdot \left[\prod_{j=1}^{n}\bar{m}_{\Theta,j}(Z_i)\right] \\[2ex] \rho = \left[\sum_{k=1}^{N}\prod_{j=1}^{n}\left(m_{k,j}(Z_i) + \bar{m}_{\Theta,j}(Z_i) + \tilde{m}_{\Theta,j}(Z_i)\right) - (N-1) \cdot \prod_{j=1}^{n}\left(\bar{m}_{\Theta,j}(Z_i) + \tilde{m}_{\Theta,j}\right)(Z_i)\right]^{-1} \\[2ex] m_{k,j}^{-}(Z_i) \le m_{k,j}(Z_i) \le m_{k,j}^{+}(Z_i), k = 1, \cdots, N \\[1ex] \bar{m}_{\Theta,j}^{-}(Z_i) \le \bar{m}_{\Theta,j}(Z_i) \le \bar{m}_{\Theta,j}^{+}(Z_i) \\[1ex] \tilde{m}_{\Theta,j}^{-}(Z_i) \le \tilde{m}_{\Theta,j}(Z_i) \le \tilde{m}_{\Theta,j}^{+}(Z_i) \\[1ex] \sum_{k=1}^{N} m_{k,j}(Z_i) + \bar{m}_{H,j}(Z_i) + \tilde{m}_{H,j}(Z_i) = 1 \end{cases}$$

$$\tag{5.6}$$

Suppose that the optimal solutions of the above pair of nonlinear programming models are $\beta_k(Z_i)^-$ and $\beta_k(Z_i)^+$, then the fused interval-valued belief degree of alternative Z_i is expressed by $[\beta_k(Z_i)^-, \beta_k(Z_i)^+]$, representing the belief degree of alternative Z_i belonging to grade H_k. Moreover, it should be highlighted that if the objective function is replaced with $\beta_\Theta(Z_i) = m_\Theta(Z_i)/(1 - \bar{m}_\Theta(Z_i))$, then the optimal solutions of the nonlinear programming models will be the fused unassigned belief degree and can be denoted by $[\beta_\Theta(Z_i)^-, \beta_\Theta(Z_i)^+]$. Generate the expected utilities of alternatives.

Once the fused interval-valued belief degrees of alternatives are obtained, the expected utilities of alternatives can be calculated to compare and rank them. Because the belief degrees are expressed by interval values, the expected utilities should also be interval values. The following nonlinear programming models are constructed to calculate the lower and upper bounds of the expected utility, respectively.

The upper bound of the expected utility can be calculated by:

$$\max u(Z_i) = \sum_{k=1}^{N} \beta_k(Z_i) \cdot u(H_k) + \beta_\Theta(Z_i) \cdot u(H_N)$$

$$s.t. \begin{cases} \beta_k(Z_i) = \dfrac{m_k(Z_i)}{1 - \bar{m}_\Theta(Z_i)} \\[2mm] m_k(Z_i) = \rho \cdot \left[\prod_{j=1}^{n} \left(m_{k,j}(Z_i) + \bar{m}_{\Theta,j}(Z_i) + \tilde{m}_{\Theta,j}(Z_i) \right) - \prod_{j=1}^{n} \left(\bar{m}_{\Theta,j}(Z_i) + \tilde{m}_{\Theta,j}(Z_i) \right) \right] \\[2mm] \tilde{m}_\Theta(Z_i) = \rho \cdot \left[\prod_{j=1}^{n} \left(\bar{m}_{\Theta,j}(Z_i) + \tilde{m}_{\Theta,j}(Z_i) \right) - \prod_{j=1}^{n} \bar{m}_{\Theta,j}(Z_i) \right] \\[2mm] \bar{m}_\Theta(Z_i) = \rho \cdot \left[\prod_{j=1}^{n} \bar{m}_{\Theta,j}(Z_i) \right] \\[2mm] \rho = \left[\sum_{k=1}^{N} \prod_{j=1}^{n} \left(m_{k,j}(Z_i) + \bar{m}_{\Theta,j}(Z_i) + \tilde{m}_{\Theta,j}(Z_i) \right) - (N-1) \cdot \prod_{j=1}^{n} \left(\bar{m}_{\Theta,j}(Z_i) + \tilde{m}_{\Theta,j}(Z_i) \right) \right]^{-1} \\[2mm] w_j^- \cdot \beta_{k,j}^-(Z_i) \le m_{k,j} \le w_j^+ \cdot \beta_{k,j}^+(Z_i) \\[2mm] 1 - w_j^+ \le \bar{m}_{\Theta,j}(Z_i) \le 1 - w_j^- \\[2mm] \sum_{k=1}^{N} m_{k,j}(Z_i) + \bar{m}_{\Theta,j}(Z_i) + \tilde{m}_{\Theta,j}(Z_i) = 1 \end{cases}$$

$$(5.7)$$

Similarly, the lower bound of the expected utility can be calculated by:

$$\min u(Z_i) = \sum_{k=1}^{N} \beta_k(Z_i) \cdot u(H_k) + \beta_\Theta(Z_i) \cdot u(H_1)$$

$$s.t. \begin{cases} \beta_k(Z_i) = \dfrac{m_k(Z_i)}{1 - \tilde{m}_\Theta(Z_i)} \\[2mm] m_k(Z_i) = \rho \cdot \left[\displaystyle\prod_{j=1}^{n} \left(m_{k,j}(Z_i) + \bar{m}_{\Theta,j}(Z_i) + \tilde{m}_{\Theta,j}(Z_i) \right) - \prod_{j=1}^{n} \left(\bar{m}_{\Theta,j}(Z_i) + \tilde{m}_{\Theta,j}(Z_i) \right) \right] \\[2mm] \tilde{m}_\Theta(Z_i) = \rho \cdot \left[\displaystyle\prod_{j=1}^{n} \left(\bar{m}_{\Theta,j}(Z_i) + \tilde{m}_{\Theta,j}(Z_i) \right) - \prod_{j=1}^{n} \bar{m}_{\Theta,j}(Z_i) \right] \\[2mm] \bar{m}_\Theta(Z_i) = \rho \cdot \left[\displaystyle\prod_{j=1}^{n} \bar{m}_{\Theta,j}(Z_i) \right] \\[2mm] \rho = \left[\displaystyle\sum_{k=1}^{N}\prod_{j=1}^{n} \left(m_{k,j}(Z_i) + \bar{m}_{\Theta,j}(Z_i) + \tilde{m}_{\Theta,j}(Z_i) \right) - (N-1) \cdot \prod_{j=1}^{n} \left(\bar{m}_{\Theta,j}(Z_i) + \tilde{m}_{\Theta,j}(Z_i) \right) \right]^{-1} \\[2mm] w_j^- \cdot \beta_{k,j}^-(Z_i) \le m_{k,j}(Z_i) \le w_j^+ \cdot \beta_{k,j}^+(Z_i) \\[2mm] 1 - w_j^+ \le \bar{m}_{\Theta,j}(Z_i) \le 1 - w_j^- \\[2mm] \displaystyle\sum_{k=1}^{N} m_{k,j}(Z_i) + \bar{m}_{\Theta,j}(Z_i) + \tilde{m}_{\Theta,j}(Z_i) = 1 \end{cases}$$

$$(5.8)$$

Suppose that the optimal solutions of the above two nonlinear programming models are denoted by $u(Z_i)^-$ and $u(Z_i)^+$, then the expected utility of the alternative Z_i can be represented by $[u(Z_i)^-, u(Z_i)^+]$.

5.3.4 AN IMPROVED MINIMAX REGRET APPROACH

Since the obtained expected utilities are characterized by interval values and cannot be directly compared and ranked, this subsection proposes a new interval-valued ranking approach based on the minimax regret approach [31]. The specific implementation processes of the proposed approach are provided below.

Suppose that there are m interval-valued expected utilities $u(Z_i) = [u(Z_i)^-, u(Z_i)^+]$, $i = 1, \ldots, m$ and $u(Z_l) = [u(Z_l)^-, u(Z_l)^+]$ represents the final selected interval-valued expected utility. If $u(Z_l)^- < \max_{i \ne l} \left\{ u(Z_i)^+ \right\}$, the decision maker may feel regret/loss, and the maximum regret degree can be calculated by:

$$\mathrm{MR}\left(u(Z_i)\right) = \max \left\{ \max_{i \ne l} u(Z_i)^+ - u(Z_l)^-, 0 \right\}$$

It is evident that the interval-valued expected utility with the minimum maximum regret degree should be regarded as the optimal interval-valued expected utility. This rule can be embodied by the following mathematical expression:

$$\min_{l}\left\{\mathrm{MR}\left(u\left(Z_{l}\right)\right)\right\} = \min_{l}\left\{\max\left\{\max_{i\neq l}\left\{u\left(Z_{i}\right)^{+}\right\} - u\left(Z_{l}\right)^{-},0\right\}\right\}$$

If there are several interval-valued expected utilities with the same minimum maximum regret degree, they can be further compared by the maximum secondary regret degree (MSR), which can be generated by the following rule.

Suppose that there are m' ($m' \leq m$) interval-valued expected utilities that have the same minimax regret degree and $u(Z_t) = [u(Z_t)^-, u(Z_t)^+]$ is the final selected interval-valued expected utility. The maximum secondary regret degree can be calculated by:

$$\mathrm{MSR}\left(u\left(Z_{t}\right)\right) = \max\left\{\max_{g\neq t}\left\{u\left(Z_{g}\right)^{+}\right\} - u\left(Z_{t}\right)^{-},0\right\}$$

Obviously, the interval-valued expected utility with the minimum maximum secondary regret degree should be selected as the optimal interval-valued expected utility, which can be embodied by the following mathematical expression:

$$\min_{t}\left\{\mathrm{MSR}\left(u\left(Z_{t}\right)\right)\right\} = \min_{t}\left\{\max\left\{\max_{g\neq t}\left\{u\left(Z_{g}\right)^{+}\right\} - u\left(Z_{t}\right)^{-},0\right\}\right\}$$

The proposed interval-valued ranking approach can be summarized as follows:

(i) If $\min\{\mathrm{MR}(u(Z_l))\} < \min\{\mathrm{MR}(u(Z_i))\}(i, l = 1, \ldots, m; l \neq i)$, then the interval-valued expected utility $u(Z_l)$ is better than $u(Z_i)$.

(ii) If $\min\{\mathrm{MPR}(u(Z_l))\} = \min\{\mathrm{MPR}(u(Z_t))\} < \min\{\mathrm{MPR}(u(Z_i))\}(l \neq t \neq i; t, l = 1, \ldots, m)$, then the maximum secondary regret degrees of $u(Z_l) = [u(Z_l)^-, u(Z_l)^+]$ and $u(Z_t) = [u(Z_t)^-, u(Z_t)^+]$ should be calculated to further distinguish $u(Z_l)$ and $u(Z_t)$, which will involve the following three situations.

Situation 1:   If $\min\{\mathrm{MSR}(u(Z_l))\} < \min\{\mathrm{MSR}(u(Z_t))\}(l \neq t; l, t = 1, \ldots, m)$, then $u(Z_l)$ is better than $u(Z_t)$ and the ranking order of the three interval-valued expected utilities is $u(Z_l) \succ u(Z_t) \succ u(Z_i)$.

Situation 2:   If $\min\{\mathrm{MSR}(u(Z_l))\} > \min\{\mathrm{MSR}(u(Z_t))\}(l \neq t; l, t = 1, \ldots, m)$, then $u(Z_l)$ is worse than $u(Z_t)$ and the ranking order of the three interval-valued expected utilities is $u(Z_t) \succ u(Z_l) \succ u(Z_i)$.

Situation 3:   If $\min\{\mathrm{MSR}(u(Z_l))\} = \min\{\mathrm{MSR}(u(Z_t))\}(l \neq t; l, t = 1, \ldots, m)$, then $u(Z_l)$ is equal to $u(Z_t)$ and the ranking order of the three interval-valued expected utilities is $u(Z_t) \approx u(Z_l) \succ u(Z_i)$.

5.4 CASE STUDY

To illustrate the performance of the proposed decision method, a case study about NEVs purchasing is provided. The evaluation information related to NEVs purchasing is collected from OTRs. Afterward, the advantages of the proposed method are discussed and explained through comparative analysis.

5.4.1 PROBLEM DESCRIPTION

With the intensification of the energy crisis and environmental pollution, NEVs have received more and more attention. China is the largest energy consumer, so it is particularly important to develop NEVs. In October 2020, the general office of the State Council issued the "new energy vehicle industry development plan (2021–2035)." The plan points out that the development of NEVs is the necessary way for China to move from a big automobile country to a powerful automobile country, and is a strategic measure to deal with climate change and promote green development. In the following 15 years, we should focus on developing NEV technology and improving the industrial layout of NEVs, and strive to make NEVs the mainstream of vehicle sales by 2035. The release of the new energy vehicle industry development plan (2021–2035) has brought a new wave of sales boom for NEVs. In the process of purchasing NEVs, many alternatives and conflicting criteria are often involved. To select the optimal alternative, it is necessary to evaluate the performance of different NEVs under these conflicting criteria. With the development of Internet 2.0 and the popularity of intelligent terminal equipment, automobile forums are becoming more and more popular. Through these automobile forums, people can express their opinions and feelings about various electric vehicles anytime and anywhere, providing an important data source for solving the evaluation problems of electric vehicles.

Automobile home (http://www.autohome.com.cn/) is a mainstream automobile Internet platform in China, providing consumers with a large amount of valuable OTR information. This subsection collects the online reviews related to NEVs on Automobile home through the crawler tool based on the scrapy framework [36]. Four popular NEVs (TESLA Model 3, NIO ES6, XPENG-P7, and BYD-Tang) are selected to demonstrate and explain this process. The collected online reviews are as follows: 546 online reviews on TESLA Model 3, 1273 online reviews on NIO ES6, 121 online reviews related to XPENG-P7, and 2718 online reviews on BYD-Tang. Five criteria (power, space, comfort, appearance, and cost performance) are derived from these collected online reviews. For the sake of simplicity, these four NEVs and five criteria are expressed by notations Z_1, Z_2, Z_3, Z_4, and C_1, C_2, C_3, C_4, C_5, respectively.

5.4.2 IMPLEMENTATION PROCESS

We herein implement the proposed decision-making method to solve the above NEVs evaluation problem, which consists mainly of the following stages.

(1) Transform the unstructured online reviews into interval-valued distribution assessment vector.

TABLE 5.1

Linguistic Distributed Information Matrix with Interval-Valued Belief Degrees

	Z_1	Z_2	Z_3	Z_4
C_1	Pos, [0.172, 0.472]; Neu, [0.258, 0.558]; Neg, [0.163, 0.463]	Pos, [0.366, 0.566]; Neu, [0.258, 0.458]; Neg, [0.132, 0.332]	Pos, [0.236, 0.336]; Neu, [0.345, 0.445]; Neg, [0.232, 0.332]	Pos, [0.163, 0.463]; Neu, [0.108, 0.408]; Neg, [0.452, 0.852]
C_2	Pos, [0.328, 0.478]; Neu, [0.254, 0.404]; Neg, [0.162, 0.312]	Pos, [0.116, 0.366]; Neu, [0.232, 0.482]; Neg, [0.162, 0.412]	Pos, [0.108, 0.308]; Neu, [0.245, 0.445]; Neg, [0.267, 0.467]	Pos, [0.242, 0.342]; Neu, [0.341, 0.441]; Neg, [0.223, 0.323]
C_3	Pos, [0.118, 0.268]; Neu, [0.354, 0.504]; Neg, [0.262, 0.412]	Pos, [0.138, 0.338]; Neu, [0.246, 0.446]; Neg, [0.337, 0.537]	Pos, [0.285, 0.385]; Neu, [0.328, 0.428]; Neg, [0.336, 0.436]	Pos, [0.332, 0.432]; Neu, [0.452, 0.552]; Neg, [0.062, 0.162]
C_4	Pos, [0.262, 0.362]; Neu, [0.158, 0.258]; Neg, [0.363, 0.463]	Pos, [0.224, 0.374]; Neu, [0.208, 0.358]; Neg, [0.346, 0.496]	Pos, [0.268, 0.568]; Neu, [0.255, 0.555]; Neg, [0.062, 0.362]	Pos, [0.438, 0.588]; Neu, [0.183, 0.333]; Neg, [0.137, 0.387]
C_5	Pos, [0.345, 0.445]; Neu, [0.254, 0.354]; Neg, [0.265, 0.365]	Pos, [0.326, 0.426]; Neu, [0.247, 0.347]; Neg, [0.332, 0.432]	Pos, [0.342, 0.492]; Neu, [0.241, 0.391]; Neg, [0.068, 0.218]	Pos, [0.342, 0.542]; Neu, [0.287, 0.487]; Neg, [0.078, 0.278]

According to the proposed distributed structure-based online review processing mechanism, the collected online reviews are transformed into linguistic distributed information with interval-valued belief degrees, as shown in Table 5.1.

To follow a CWW scheme, the sentiment words (positive, neutral, and negative) in Table 5.1 are transformed into IT2FSs. The corresponding relationships between sentiment words and IT2FSs are provided below.

$$\text{Positive}: \left[(7.2, 8.6, 9, 9.6, 1); (8, 8.8, 8.8, 9.2, 0.9) \right];$$

$$\text{Neutral}: \left[(5.8, 6.6, 7.8, 8.8, 1); (6.2, 7.4, 7.4, 8, 0.9) \right];$$

$$\text{Negative}: \left[(0.8, 3.6, 5.8, 7.2, 1); (1.2, 4.4, 4.4, 5.6, 0.9) \right].$$

(2) Calculate the criteria weights of NEVs evaluation problem

First, based on the obtained linguistic distributed information matrix and IT2FSs, as shown in Table 5.2.

Second, the interval-valued entropy of each criterion can be calculated. The results are summarized in Table 5.3.

Then, the interval-valued dispersion of each criterion can be generated. The corresponding results are summarized in Table 5.4.

(3) Finally, the interval-valued criteria weights can be generated according to Eq. (5.3). The corresponding results are $w_1 = [0.733, 1]$, $w_2 = [0.364, 0.5]$, $w_3 = [0.25, 0.333]$, $w_4 = [0.19, 0.25]$, and $w_5 = [0.156, 0.2]$. Fuse the interval type-2 fuzzy distributed information

TABLE 5.2
Score Value of Linguistic Distributed Information

	Z_1	Z_2	Z_3	Z_4
C_1	[1.36, 3.64]	[1.89, 3.43]	[1.86, 2.72]	[1.36, 3.89]
C_2	[1.81, 3]	[1.13, 3.05]	[1.28, 2.87]	[1.85, 2.71]
C_3	[1.58, 2.81]	[1.47, 3.08]	[2.1, 3]	[2.17, 3]
C_4	[1.65, 2.54]	[1.64, 2.89]	[1.5, 3.75]	[1.92, 3.27]
C_5	[2, 2.86]	[2.02, 2.9]	[1.69, 2.85]	[1.82, 3.35]

TABLE 5.3
Interval-Valued Entropy of Each Criterion

	C_1	C_2	C_3	C_4	C_5
E_j	[0.811, 0.861]	[0.808, 0.861]	[0.828, 0.861]	[0.825, 0.861]	[0.843, 0.861]

TABLE 5.4
Interval-Valued Dispersion of Each Criterion

	C_1	C_2	C_3	C_4	C_5
ξ_j	[0.139, 0.189]	[0.139, 0.192]	[0.139, 0.172]	[0.139, 0.175]	[0.139, 0.157]

First, according to Eqs. (5.1)–(5.5), the distributed information is transformed into basic probability masses. Due to space limitation, we only take the interval-valued belief degree of alternative Z_1 under criterion C_1 assigned to grade H_1 as an example. The results are provided below.

$$m_{1,1}(Z_1) = [0.027, 0.094]$$
$$\tilde{m}_{\Theta,1}(Z_1) = [0, 0.08]$$
$$\bar{m}_{\Theta,1} = [0, 0.267]$$

Then, the fused interval-valued belief degree of each alternative can be generated by Eq. (5.6) and the results are summarized in Table 5.5.

Finally, the interval-valued expected utilities of alternatives can be generated by Eqs. (5.7 and 5.8), the results are shown in Table 5.6.

(4) Compare and rank the interval-valued expected utilities

First, calculate the maximum regret degree of each interval-valued expected utility.

TABLE 5.5
Interval-Valued Belief Degree of Each Alternative

	Pos	Neu	Neg
Z_1	[0.125, 0.424]	[0.134, 0.387]	[0.142, 0.379]
Z_2	[0.112, 0.43]	[0.126, 0.389]	[0.134, 0.391]
Z_3	[0.106, 0.427]	[0.135, 0.401]	[0.123, 0.374]
Z_4	[0.132, 0.447]	[0.135, 0.401]	[0.123, 0.374]

TABLE 5.6
Interval-Valued Dispersion of Each Criterion

	Z_1	Z_2	Z_3	Z_4
$u(Z_i)$	[0.209, 0.303]	[0.197, 0.29]	[0.191, 0.285]	[0.2, 0.294]

$$\text{MR}\left(u\left(Z_1\right)\right) = \max\left[\max\left\{0.29, 0.285, 0.294\right\} - 0.209, 0\right] = 0.085$$

$$\text{MR}\left(u\left(Z_2\right)\right) = \max\left[\max\left\{0.303, 0.285, 0.294\right\} - 0.197, 0\right] = 0.106$$

$$\text{MR}\left(u\left(Z_3\right)\right) = \max\left[\max\left\{0.303, 0.289, 0.294\right\} - 0.191, 0\right] = 0.112$$

$$\text{MR}\left(u\left(Z_4\right)\right) = \max\left[\max\left\{0.303, 0.289, 0.285\right\} - 0.2, 0\right] = 0.103$$

From the results, we can find that Z_1, that is, TESLA Model 3 has the minimum maximum regret degree. Therefore, TESLA Model 3 is selected as the optimal alternative.

Then, calculate the maximum regret degree of each remaining interval-valued expected utility.

$$\text{MR}\left(u\left(Z_2\right)\right) = \max\left[\max\left\{0.285, 0.294\right\} - 0.197, 0\right] = 0.097$$

$$\text{MR}\left(u\left(Z_3\right)\right) = \max\left[\max\left\{0.289, 0.294\right\} - 0.191, 0\right] = 0.103$$

$$\text{MR}\left(u\left(Z_4\right)\right) = \max\left[\max\left\{0.289, 0.285\right\} - 0.2, 0\right] = 0.089$$

The alternative Z_4, that is, BYD-Tang is selected as the second alternative.

Finally, the maximum regret degrees of alternatives Z_2 and Z_3 are calculated.

$$\text{MR}\left(u\left(Z_2\right)\right) = \max\left[0.285 - 0.197, 0\right] = 0.088$$

$$\text{MR}\left(u\left(Z_3\right)\right) = \max\left[0.289 - 0.191, 0\right] = 0.098$$

From the above analysis, we can conclude that the ranking order of the four alternatives is $Z_1 > Z_4 > Z_3 > Z_2$.

5.5   CONCLUSIONS

This study proposed an interval type-2 decision analysis framework based on OTRs. First, considering the unstructured characteristics and individual differences of the text reviews, this study presents an interval type-2 distributed structure-based processing mechanism for the OTRs. Through this mechanism, the unstructured information is transformed into distributed information with interval-valued belief degrees. Second, to determine the criteria weights, an entropy-based interval type-2 fuzzy weights determination model is provided. The criteria weights are characterized by interval values, which can better describe the uncertainty of the criteria. Then, an ER-based information fusion approach is proposed to calculate the interval-valued expected utility of each alternative. Since the expected utilities are expressed by interval values, an improved minimax regret approach is developed to compare and rank the interval-valued expected utilities. Finally, a case study related to NEVs evaluation has been provided to show the effectiveness of the proposed method.

REFERENCES

[1] J. Surowiecki, *The Wisdom of Crowds*, Knopf Doubleday Publishing Group, 2005. URL https://books.google.es/books?id=hHUsHOHqVzEC

[2] G. Carvalho, A. S. Vivacqua, J. M. Souza, S. P. J. Medeiros, LaSca: a large scale group decision support system, *Journal of Universal Computer Science* 17 (2) (2011) 261–275.

[3] D. García-Zamora, Á. Labella, W. Ding, R. M. Rodríguez, L. Martínez, Large-scale group decision making: a systematic review and a critical analysis, *IEEE/CAA Journal of Automatica Sinica* 9 (6) (2022) 949–966. doi:10.1109/JAS.2022.105617

[4] I. Song, Y. Zhu, Big data and data science: what should we teach?, *Expert Systems* 33 (4) (2016) 364–373.

[5] C. Zuheros, E. Martinez-Camara, E. Herrera-Viedma, F. Herrera, Crowd decision making: sparse representation guided by sentiment analysis for leveraging the wisdom of the crowd, *IEEE Transactions on Systems, Man, and Cybernetics: Systems* (2022) 1–11 doi:10.1109/TSMC.2022.3180938

[6] H. Fadili, C. Jouis, Towards an automatic analyze and standardization of unstructured data in the context of big and linked data, in: *Proceedings of the 8th International Conference on Management of Digital EcoSystems*, 2016, pp. 223–230.

[7] J. Yang, Y. Wang, D. Xu, K. Chin, The evidential reasoning approach for mada under both probabilistic and fuzzy uncertainties, *European Journal of Operational Research* 171 (1) (2006) 309–343.

[8] M. Guo, J. Yang, K. Chin, H. Wang, X. Liu, Evidential reasoning approach for multiattribute decision analysis under both fuzzy and interval uncertainty, *IEEE Transactions on Fuzzy Systems* 17 (3) (2008) 683–697.

[9] G. Zhang, Y. Dong, Y. Xu, Consistency and consensus measures for linguistic preference relations based on distribution assessments, *Information Fusion* 17 (2014) 46–55.

[10] J. Yang, D. Xu, On the evidential reasoning algorithm for multiple attribute decision analysis under uncertainty, *IEEE Transactions on Systems, Man, and Cybernetics-Part A: Systems and Humans* 32 (3) (2002) 289–304.

[11] J. M. Mendel, R. B. John, Type-2 fuzzy sets made simple, *IEEE Transactions on Fuzzy Systems* 10 (2) (2002) 117–127.

[12] Y. Wang, J. Yang, D. Xu, K. Chin, The evidential reasoning approach for multiple attribute decision analysis using interval belief degrees, *European Journal of Operational Research* 175 (1) (2006) 35–66.

[13] J. M. Mendel, R. I. John, F. Liu, Interval type-2 fuzzy logic systems made simple, *IEEE Transactions on Fuzzy Systems* 14 (6) (2006) 808–821.

[14] J. M. Mendel, H. Wu, Type-2 fuzzistics for symmetric interval type-2 fuzzy sets: part 1, forward problems, *IEEE Transactions on Fuzzy Systems* 14 (6) (2006) 781–792.

[15] L. A. Zadeh, The concept of a linguistic variable and its application to approximate reasoning—i, *Information Sciences* 8 (3) (1975) 199–249.

[16] R. Boukezzoula, D. Coquin, A decision-making computational methodology for a class of type-2 fuzzy intervals: an interval-based approach, *Information Sciences* 510 (2020) 256–282.

[17] X. Pan, Y. Wang, An enhanced technique for order preference by similarity to ideal solutions and its application to renewable energy resources selection problem, *International Journal of Fuzzy Systems* 23 (4) (2021) 1087–1101.

[18] X. Pan, Y. Wang, Evaluation of renewable energy sources in china using an interval type-2 fuzzy large-scale group risk evaluation method, *Applied Soft Computing* 108 (2021) 107458.

[19] J. Qin, X. Liu, W. Pedrycz, An extended todim multi-criteria group decision making method for green supplier selection in interval type-2 fuzzy environment, *European Journal of Operational Research* 258 (2) (2017) 626–638.

[20] P. Kundu, S. Kar, M. Maiti, A fuzzy multi-criteria group decision making based on ranking interval type-2 fuzzy variables and an application to transportation mode selection problem, *Soft Computing* 21 (11) (2017) 3051–3062.

[21] S. Chen, Y. Chang, Fuzzy interpolative reasoning based on the footprints of uncertainty of interval type-2 fuzzy sets, in: *2010 International Conference on Computational Aspects of Social Networks*, IEEE, 2010, pp. 569–572.

[22] T. Chen, An electre-based outranking method for multiple criteria group decision making using interval type-2 fuzzy sets, *Information Sciences* 263 (2014) 1–21.

[23] T. Chen, An interval type-2 fuzzy promethee method using a likelihood-based outranking comparison approach, *Information Fusion* 25 (2015) 105–120.

[24] Y. Wu, J. Wang, Y. Hu, Y. Ke, L. Li, An extended todim-promethee method for waste-to-energy plant site selection based on sustainability perspective, *Energy* 156 (2018) 1–16.

[25] T. Bao, X. Xie, P. Long, Z. Wei, Madm method based on prospect theory and evidential reasoning approach with unknown attribute weights under intuitionistic fuzzy environment, *Expert Systems with Applications* 88 (2017) 305–317.

[26] D. Liang, M. Wang, Z. Xu, D. Liu, Risk appetite dual hesitant fuzzy three-way decisions with todim, *Information Sciences* 507 (2020) 585–605.

[27] S. Narayanamoorthy, S. Geetha, R. Rakkiyappan, Y. H. Joo, Interval-valued intuitionistic hesitant fuzzy entropy based vikor method for industrial robots selection, *Expert Systems with Applications* 121 (2019) 28–37.

[28] J. Yang, M. G. Singh, An evidential reasoning approach for multiple-attribute decision making with uncertainty, *IEEE Transactions on Systems, Man, and Cybernetics* 24 (1) (1994) 1–18.

[29] A. P. Dempster, Upper and lower probabilities induced by a multivalued mapping, in: *Classic Works of the Dempster-Shafer Theory of Belief Functions*, Springer, 2008, pp. 57–72.

[30] Y. Wang, J. Yang, D. Xu, Environmental impact assessment using the evidential reasoning approach, *European Journal of Operational Research* 174 (3) (2006) 1885–1913.

[31] M. Zhang, Y. Wang, L. Li, S. Chen, A general evidential reasoning algorithm for multi-attribute decision analysis under interval uncertainty, *European Journal of Operational Research* 257 (3) (2017) 1005–1015.

[32] J. Lan, H. Zou, M. Hu, Dominance degrees for intervals and their application in multiple attribute decision-making, *Fuzzy Sets and Systems* 383 (2020) 146–164.

[33] S. Kundu, Min-transitivity of fuzzy leftness relationship and its application to decision making, *Fuzzy Sets and Systems* 86 (3) (1997) 357–367.

[34] Y. Wang, R. Greatbanks, J. Yang, Interval efficiency assessment using data envelopment analysis, *Fuzzy Sets and Systems* 153 (3) (2005) 347–370.

[35] P. Liu, F. Teng, Probabilistic linguistic todim method for selecting products through online product reviews, *Information Sciences* 485 (2019) 441–455.

[36] S. He, Y. Wang, X. Pan, K. Chin, Decision analysis framework based on incomplete online textual reviews, *Information Sciences* 584 (2022) 701–718.

[37] D. Wu, J. M. Mendel, S. Coupland, Enhanced interval approach for encoding words into interval type-2 fuzzy sets and its convergence analysis, *IEEE Transactions on Fuzzy Systems* 20 (3) (2011) 499–513.

[38] X. Pan, Y. Wang, S. He, A new regret theory-based risk decision-making method for renewable energy investment under uncertain environment, *Computers & Industrial Engineering* 170 (2022) 108319.

[39] L. Wang, Y.-M. Wang, L. Martinez, A group decision method based on prospect theory for emergency situations, *Information Sciences* 418 (2017) 119–135.

[40] X. Pan, Y. Wang, S. He, The evidential reasoning approach for renewable energy resources evaluation under interval type-2 fuzzy uncertainty, *Information Sciences* 576 (2021) 432–453.

[41] X. Pan, Y. Wang, S. He, K.-S. Chin, A dynamic programming algorithm based clustering model and its application to interval type-2 fuzzy large-scale group decision-making problem, *IEEE Transactions on Fuzzy Systems* 30 (1) (2020) 108–120.

[42] F. Torfi, R. Z. Farahani, S. Rezapour, Fuzzy AHP to determine the relative weights of evaluation criteria and fuzzy topsis to rank the alternatives, *Applied Soft Computing* 10 (2) (2010) 520–528.

[43] Y. Wu, Y. Ke, C. Xu, L. Li, An integrated decision-making model for sustainable photovoltaic module supplier selection based on combined weight and cumulative prospect theory, *Energy* 181 (2019) 1235–1251.

[44] M. Irfan, R. M. Elavarasan, M. Ahmad, M. Mohsin, V. Dagar, Y. Hao, Prioritizing and overcoming biomass energy barriers: application of AHP and G-TOPSIS approaches, *Technological Forecasting and Social Change* 177 (2022) 121524.

[45] F. Lolli, A. M. Coruzzolo, E. Balugani, The indoor environmental quality: a topsis-based approach with indirect elicitation of criteria weights, *Safety Science* 148 (2022) 105652.

6 Robust Comprehensive Minimum Cost Consensus Model for Multi-Criteria Group Decision Making
Application in IoT Platform Selection

Yefan Han
Shanghai University, Shanghai, China
Universidad de Jaén, Jaén, Spain

Bapi Dutta, Diego García-Zamora and Luis Martínez
Universidad de Jaén, Jaén, Spain

6.1 INTRODUCTION

With the increasing complexity of the decision-making environment, decisions based on an alternative evaluation (one criterion) may no longer be applicable (Xu, Du, & Chen, 2015). In addition, due to the limited individuals' cognition and knowledge, many practical decision problems are often solved in a group setting, in which multiple independent experts in related fields take part (García-Zamora et al., 2022b). Therefore, multi-criteria group decision-making (MCGDM) problems have attracted a lot of attention from researchers (Ben-Arieh & Easton, 2007; Xu et al., 2015). They can be described as a process in which multiple experts evaluate feasible alternatives according to multiple criteria and then select the optimal alternative (Zhong, Xu, & Pan, 2022). Recently, MCGDM has been successfully applied to many practical decision problems in different fields, such as green supplier selection, product development, engineering project management, emergencies, etc. (Büyüközkan & Güleryüz, 2016; Fu, Chang, & Yang, 2020; Qin, Liu, & Pedrycz, 2017; Xu, Yin, & Chen, 2019).

In general, experts involved in decision making usually come from different groups of interest and differ in terms of educational background, knowledge

DOI: 10.1201/9781003340621-6

structure, professional references, understanding and concerns. In such a context, the emergence of disagreements among experts is inevitable. Therefore, applying a consensus reaching process (CRP) before ranking the alternatives is indispensable (Nie et al., 2020). In a CRP, experts discuss and modify their preferences with the aim of increasing the agreement level among themselves (Palomares, Martinez, & Herrera, 2013; Xu et al., 2015). Consensus has different interpretations, ranging from the unanimous agreement within groups to a more flexible soft consensus (Fedrizzi, Fedrizzi, & Pereira, 1999; Kacprzyk, 1986; Zhang, Kou, & Peng, 2019), which is usually calculated based on two consensus measures (Tian et al., 2020; Zhong et al., 2022): (1) The distance between an individual's opinions and the collective (Nie et al., 2020) and (2) the distance between individuals' opinions (Wu & Xu, 2016).

Developing a CRP involves the adjustment of the experts' initial opinions. However, each expert wants his/her opinion to be seriously taken into account, and sometimes they may be reluctant to adjust their preferences (Rodríguez et al., 2021). Several researchers have pointed out the importance of considering the cost of modifying experts' opinions to reach consensus, which has become an attractive challenge in the CRP literature (Ben-Arieh & Easton, 2007; Labella et al., 2020; Zhang, Dong, & Xu, 2013).

Ben-Arieh and Easton (2007) first defined the concept of minimum cost consensus (6.1) models as automatic CRPs in which the cost of modifying experts' preferences is minimized subject to a consensus constraint. Dong et al. (2010) used this idea to develop a minimum adjustment model in a linguistic setting, and Zhang et al. (2011) introduced aggregation operators and built an MCC model based on a linear cost function. Subsequently, a large number of new MCC models were proposed (Gong et al., 2015; Zhang et al., 2018; Zhang, Gong & Chiclana, 2017). Labella et al. (2020) pointed out that these MCC models only considered a maximum distance between each expert's preference and the collective opinion, and neglected the classical consensus measures (Rodríguez et al., 2018). To overcome this limitation, Labella et al. (2020) introduced the comprehensive minimum cost (6.2) models. However, these models only consider cases where the preference structure is either a numerical utility value or a fuzzy preference relation, and they are not applicable to MCGDM problems with multiple evaluation criteria.

Furthermore, all the above MCC models assume that the cost of modifying experts' opinions is precisely determined. However, in real decision problems, obtaining the exact adjustment cost of each expert may be very difficult due to their uncertain nature (Han et al., 2019; Li, Zhang & Dong, 2017). In this sense, robust optimization (RO) is an emerging method for dealing with uncertain optimization problems, and it has been widely used in various fields for its ability to generate uncertainty-immune solutions (Chakrabarti, 2021; Kuhn et al., 2019; Qu et al., 2021). Compared to traditional uncertainty optimization methods, RO has the following advantages:

- RO methods take uncertainty into account in the modeling process, describe uncertain parameters in the form of an uncertainty set and limit their perturbation range (Han et al., 2019).

- RO does not require obtaining the exact distribution information or fuzzy affiliation functions of uncertain parameters in advance, which is not possible for stochastic or fuzzy programming (Kuhn et al., 2019).
- The RO model is worst-oriented, and its solution satisfies all constraints while making the value of the objective function optimal under the worst-case scenario. Therefore, the RO model has strong robustness and the optimal solution is less sensitive to parameter changes (Qu et al., 2021).

In this proposal, we build a robust CMCC model for MCGDM problems. The CMCC model is first extended to the MCGDM problem. The RO method is then introduced to place the expert's unit adjustment cost in a budget uncertainty set with the aim of obtaining the optimal solution satisfying all constraints in the worst-case scenario. Finally, we show the implementation of the proposed framework in an illustrative example related to an (Internet of Things) IoT platform selection.

The remainder of this chapter is organized as follows. Section 6.2 introduces some basics about MCGDM, CRPs and MCC models. Section 6.3 develops a CMCC model for MCGDM and a robust MCGDM model considering uncertain unit adjustment costs. An illustrative example is shown in Section 6.4. Finally, Section 6.5 gives some conclusions.

6.2 PRELIMINARIES

This section introduces some basic concepts related to MCGDM, consensus models and MCC.

6.2.1 MULTI-CRITERIA GROUP DECISION MAKING

GDM aims for multiple decision-makers to reach a common solution for a decision problem consisting of several alternatives according to their own preferences. In MCGDM problems, this collective decision must be made according to different criteria. Formally, a classical MCGDM problem consists of:

- A set of alternatives, $A = \{a_1, a_2, ..., a_m\}(m \geq 2)$, from which a possible solution to the problem can be selected.
- A group of experts, $E = \{e_1, e_2, ..., e_K\}(K \geq 2)$, who express their preference on the set of alternatives A.
- A set of evaluation criteria $Q = \{q_1, q_2, ..., q_n\}$ for assessing the alternatives A in different dimensions.

Each expert expresses their assessment of the alternatives based on their own experience and knowledge. A common preference structure is the preference assessment matrix, $P = (p_{ij}) \in M([0, 1])_{m \times n}$, where $p_{ij} \in [0, 1]$ represents the evaluation value of the alternatives a_i on the criterion q_j. In order to reflect the relevance of each criterion, it is usual to consider a weighting vector $\omega = (\omega_1, \omega_2, ..., \omega_n)$, satisfying $\omega_j \geq 0, \sum_{j=1}^{n} \omega_j = 1$, where each ω_j represents the relative importance of the criterion q_j.

The solution to an MCGDM problem consists of two phases (Roubens, 1997):

- **Aggregation:** The collective opinion is obtained by fusing the experts' preference assessment matrices using an aggregation operator. The weight $W = (w_1, w_2, \ldots, w_K)$ of the experts is required for this process.
- **Exploitation:** The best alternative is selected as the solution to the decision problem based on collective preference.

However, this two-phase solution process does not guarantee that conflicts will not arise among the experts involved in the decision-making problem. To ensure a collective agreement, a CRP must be included in the resolution scheme before the final decision is made (Labella et al., 2020).

6.2.2 Consensus Reaching Process

A CRP is an iterative process in which experts attempt to make their preferences close to others through discussion and modification. This process usually requires a moderator, who represents the group's interest and provides guidance for the experts to properly modify their opinions. Group consensus can be achieved by scheduling various possible resources, such as manpower, material and financial resources, and persuading experts to change their preferences within a certain period through rational debate and negotiation. A classical CRP scheme usually contains four key aspects (see Figure 6.1) (Palomares et al., 2014):

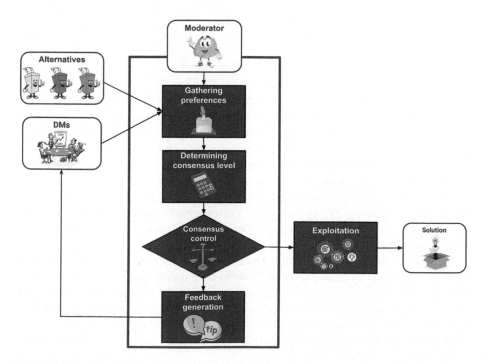

FIGURE 6.1   Scheme of a CRP.

- **Gathering preferences:** Experts' preferences are provided based on the corresponding form of preference expressions.
- **Determining consensus level:** The agreement level among experts is calculated by applying different distance measures and aggregation operators.
- **Consensus control:** The obtained agreement level is compared with a predefined consensus threshold. If the consensus level reaches the given threshold, the desired consensus has been reached and the CRP finishes; otherwise, another round of discussion process needs to be carried out.
- **Feedback generation:** A procedure to improve the consensus level through multiple rounds of discussion, in which the moderator identifies the experts causing disagreement and suggests adjustments for them. This procedure can also be performed based on automatic updates from experts.

6.2.3 MINIMUM COST CONSENSUS MODELS

In a CRP, certain costs, such as manpower, time, or money, inevitably occur. To reduce such costs, Ben-Arieh and Easton suggested that "a consensus is reached when the distance between experts and collective opinion is minimal" (2007). Formally, for the set of experts E, let $O = (o_1, o_2, ..., o_K)$ represent their initial opinions, $\overline{O} = (\overline{o}_1, \overline{o}_2, ..., \overline{o}_K)$ refer to the experts' adjusted opinions and $\overline{o}$ be the collective opinion. Let $C = (c_1, c_2, ..., c_K)$ be the unit adjustment cost of modifying experts' preferences. Then, the MCC model based on the linear cost function is as follows:

$$\min_{\overline{O} \in \mathbb{R}^K} \sum_{k=1}^{K} c_k \left| \overline{o}_k - o_k \right|$$

$$s.t. \left| \overline{o}_k - \overline{o} \right| \leq \varepsilon, k = 1, 2, ..., K \tag{6.1}$$

where ε is the maximum acceptable distance between each expert's adjusted opinion and the collective opinion. If the expert's opinion is in the interval $\left[\overline{o} - \varepsilon, \overline{o} + \varepsilon \right]$, then the expert does not need to change his/her opinion, otherwise, the expert needs to make adjustments until the distance between current opinion and $\overline{o}$ is exactly ε.

Dong et al.'s minimum adjustment consensus model provided a new perspective for the study of consensus in group decision making, which combines linguistic methods and benefits from the weighted average operator (Dong et al., 2010). Based on these investigations, Zhang et al. (2011) investigated how the aggregation operator used to fuse experts' opinions and get collective opinion that affects the calculation of the consensus level.

These models calculate the consensus degree, considering the distance between each expert and the collective opinion. However, the use of classical consensus measures to determine the consensus degree among experts was ignored. In order to ensure an acceptable consensus degree among all experts while taking into account the distance of each expert from the collective opinion, Labella et al. (2020) developed CMCC models. Such models include an additional constraint determined by a predefined consensus threshold $\alpha \in [0, 1]$ and a consensus measure $\mathbb{C} : [a, b]^K \to$ [0, 1]. Therefore, the mathematical description of the CMCC model is as follows:

$$\min_{\overline{O} \in [a,b]^K} \sum_{k=1}^{K} c_k \left| \overline{o}_k - o_k \right|$$

$$s.t. \begin{cases} \left| \overline{o}_k - \overline{o} \right| \le \varepsilon, k = 1, 2, \ldots, K \\ \overline{o} = F\left(\overline{o}_1, \overline{o}_2, \ldots, \overline{o}_K \right) \\ \mathbb{C}\left(\overline{o}_1, \overline{o}_2, \ldots, \overline{o}_K \right) \ge \alpha \end{cases} \qquad (6.2)$$

where $F(\cdot)$ is an aggregation function.

For instance, if the consensus measure is defined as $\mathbb{C}\left(\overline{o}_1, \overline{o}_2, \ldots, \overline{o}_K \right)$ $= 1 - \sum_{k=1}^{K} w_k \left| \overline{o}_k - o_k \right|$, where $w_1, w_2, \ldots, w_K \ge 0$, $\sum_{k=1}^{K} w_k = 1$, stand for the experts' relative importance, the aforementioned model is as follows:

$$\min_{\overline{O} \in [a,b]^K} \sum_{k=1}^{K} c_k \left| \overline{o}_k - o_k \right|$$

$$s.t. \begin{cases} \left| \overline{o}_k - \overline{o} \right| \le \varepsilon, k = 1, 2, \ldots, K \\ \overline{o} = \sum_{k=1}^{K} w_k \overline{o}_k \\ 1 - \sum_{k=1}^{K} w_k \left| \overline{o}_k - o_k \right| \ge \alpha \end{cases}$$

6.2.4 ROBUST OPTIMIZATION

RO method is an effective and popular tool for dealing with data uncertainty in mathematical programming models. They have received a great deal of attention because of their ability to generate uncertainty-immune solutions. The basic idea of RO is to establish a suitable uncertainty set to limit the perturbation range of uncertain parameters and generate solutions that satisfy all the constraints.

Consider the general linear programming problem:

$$\min_{x \in \mathbb{R}^{n \times 1}} c^T x$$

$$s.t. Ax \ge b \qquad (6.3)$$

where $x \in \mathbb{R}^{n \times 1}$ is the vector of the decision variable and $A \in \mathbb{R}^{m \times n}$, $b \in \mathbb{R}^{m \times 1}$ are the coefficient matrix and vector, respectively. In RO, the aim is to minimize an objective function subject to some constraints defined via uncertain parameters. For instance,

$$\min_{x \in \mathbb{R}^{n \times 1}} c^T x$$
$$s.t. Ax \geq b, \ \forall \ A, b \in \mathcal{U} \qquad\qquad (LP_{\mathcal{U}})$$

where A, b are uncertain and belong to the uncertainty set $\mathcal{U}$, which is supposed to be parameterized by a perturbation vector ξ varying in a certain perturbation set $\mathcal{Z}$.

If x is a feasible robust solution to the robust problem $(LP_{\mathcal{U}})$, it satisfies all realizations of the constraint of the uncertainty set $\mathcal{U}$. Note that the robust problem is worst-oriented, that is, the solution to $LP_{\mathcal{U}}$ is given as:

$$\min_{x \in \mathbb{R}^{n \times 1}} \left\{ \sup_{(A,b) \in \mathcal{U}} c^T x : Ax \geq b \ \forall \ A, b \in \mathcal{U} \right\}$$

which is the best robust goal value for all feasible solutions.

6.3 ROBUST COMPREHENSIVE MINIMUM COST CONSENSUS FOR MULTI-CRITERIA DECISION MAKING

This section establishes a deterministic CMCC model for the MCGDM problem. Then, a robust CMCC model for MCGDM is developed, considering the uncertainty regarding experts' unit adjustment costs.

The decision matrix is one of the most widely used preference structures in MCGDM (García-Zamora et al., 2022b). Therefore, we first need to extend the (6.2) model to manage decision matrices.

Given the decision matrices $P_k = \left(p_{ij}^k \right) \in \mathcal{M}\left([0,1] \right)_{m \times n}, k = 1, \ldots, K$, where $p_{ij}^k \in [0,1]$ represents expert e_k's evaluation for the alternative a_i with respect to the criteria q_j, let $\overline{P}_k = \left(\overline{p}_{ij}^k \right) \in \mathcal{M}\left([0,1] \right)_{m \times n}, k = 1, 2, \ldots, K$ denote the experts' adjusted preference decision matrices. The collective opinion $\overline{P} \in \mathcal{M}\left([0,1] \right)_{m \times n}$ may be computed using the weighted average (WA) operator as follows:

$$\overline{p}_{ij} = \sum_{k=1}^{K} w_k \overline{p}_{ij}^k, i = 1, \ldots, m, j = 1, \ldots, n,$$

where $w_1, \ldots, w_K$ stand for experts' weights. On the basis of this collective decision matrix, the consensus measure $\mathbb{C} : \mathcal{M}\left([0,1] \right)_{m \times n}^{K} \rightarrow [0,1]$ can be defined as follows:

$$\mathbb{C}\left(\overline{P}^1, \overline{P}^2, \ldots, \overline{P}^K \right) = 1 - \frac{1}{mn} \sum_{k=1}^{K} \sum_{i=1}^{m} \sum_{j=1}^{n} w_k \left| \overline{p}_{ij}^k - \overline{p}_{ij} \right|$$

Since we also aim to control the degree of consensus of the selected alternative after taking into account the weights of the criteria $\omega_1, \ldots, \omega_n \geq 0$, $\sum_{j=1}^{n} \omega_j = 1$, we need to introduce the following additional constraints:

$$\bar{p}_i^k = \sum_{j=1}^{n} \omega_j \bar{p}_{ij}^k, i = 1, \ldots, m, k = 1, \ldots, K$$

$$\bar{p}_i = \sum_{k=1}^{K} w_k \bar{p}_i^k, i = 1, \ldots, m$$

$$\beta \geq \left| \bar{p}_i^k - \bar{p}_i \right|, i = 1, \ldots, m, k = 1, \ldots, K$$

where $\bar{p}_i^k$ represents the score provided by the expert e_k about alternative a_i after considering all criteria, $\bar{p}_i$ is the collective score for alternative a_i and β is a threshold to control the distance between them. Therefore, the deterministic CMCC model (6.4) for MCGDM can be formulated as follows:

$$\min_{\left(\bar{p}_{ij}^k\right) \in \mathcal{M}([0,1])_{m \times n}} \sum_{k=1}^{K} \sum_{i=1}^{m} \sum_{j=1}^{n} c_k \left| \bar{p}_{ij}^k - p_{ij}^k \right|$$

$$s.t. \begin{cases} \bar{p}_{ij} = \sum_{k=1}^{K} w_k \bar{p}_{ij}^k, i = 1, \ldots, m, j = 1, \ldots, n \\[2mm] \left| \bar{p}_{ij}^k - \bar{p}_{ij} \right| \leq \varepsilon, k = 1, \ldots, K, i = 1, \ldots, m, j = 1, \ldots, n \\[2mm] 1 - \dfrac{1}{mn} \sum_{k=1}^{K} \sum_{i=1}^{m} \sum_{j=1}^{n} w_k \left| \bar{p}_{ij}^k - \bar{p}_{ij} \right| \geq \alpha \\[2mm] \bar{p}_i^k = \sum_{j=1}^{n} \omega_j \bar{p}_{ij}^k, i = 1, \ldots, m, k = 1, \ldots, K \\[2mm] \bar{p}_i = \sum_{k=1}^{K} w_k \bar{p}_i^k, i = 1, \ldots, m \\[2mm] \left| \bar{p}_i^k - \bar{p}_i \right| \leq \beta, i = 1, \ldots, m, k = 1, \ldots, K \end{cases} \tag{6.4}$$

The existence of absolute value operation increases the difficulty of solving the nonlinear model (6.4). Therefore, we transform it into an equivalent linear programming model to improve the efficiency of obtaining optimal solutions in decision-making scenarios.

Theorem 1

Model (6.4) is equivalent to the linear programming model (6.5).

$$\min_{\left(\bar{p}_{ij}^k\right)\in\mathcal{M}\left([0,1]\right)_{m\times n}} B$$

$$
s.t.\begin{cases}
\displaystyle\sum_{k=1}^{K}\sum_{i=1}^{m}\sum_{j=1}^{n}c_k z_{ij}^k \leq B \\[2ex]
\displaystyle\bar{p}_{ij} = \sum_{k=1}^{K}w_k \bar{p}_{ij}^k, i=1,\ldots,m, j=1,\ldots,n \\[2ex]
\displaystyle 1-\frac{1}{mn}\sum_{k=1}^{K}\sum_{i=1}^{m}\sum_{j=1}^{n}w_k t_{ij}^k \geq \alpha \\[2ex]
t_{ij}^k \leq \varepsilon, k=1,\ldots,K, i=1,\ldots,m, j=1,\ldots,n \\[1ex]
\displaystyle\bar{p}_i^k = \sum_{j=1}^{n}\omega_j \bar{p}_{ij}^k, i=1,\ldots,m, k=1,\ldots,K \\[2ex]
\displaystyle\bar{p}_i = \sum_{k=1}^{K}w_k \bar{p}_i^k, i=1,\ldots,m \\[2ex]
\bar{p}_{ij}^k - p_{ij}^k = y_{ij}^k, k=1,\ldots,K, i=1,\ldots,m, j=1,\ldots,n \\[1ex]
y_{ij}^k \leq z_{ij}^k, k=1,\ldots,K, i=1,\ldots,m, j=1,\ldots,n \\[1ex]
-y_{ij}^k \leq z_{ij}^k, k=1,\ldots,K, i=1,\ldots,m, j=1,\ldots,n \\[1ex]
\bar{p}_{ij}^k - \bar{p}_{ij} = s_{ij}^k, k=1,\ldots,K, i=1,\ldots,m, j=1,\ldots,n \\[1ex]
s_{ij}^k \leq t_{ij}^k, k=1,\ldots,K, i=1,\ldots,m, j=1,\ldots,n \\[1ex]
-s_{ij}^k \leq t_{ij}^k, k=1,\ldots,K, i=1,\ldots,m, j=1,\ldots,n \\[1ex]
\bar{p}_i^k - \bar{p}_i \leq \beta, i=1,\ldots,m, k=1,\ldots,K \\[1ex]
-\bar{p}_i^k + \bar{p}_i \leq \beta, i=1,\ldots,m, k=1,\ldots,K
\end{cases}
$$

(6.5)

Proof: Consider the transformation $\bar{p}_{ij}^k - p_{ij}^k = y_{ij}^k, \left|\bar{p}_{ij}^k - p_{ij}^k\right| = z_{ij}^k$. Based on the property of the absolute value $|a| = \max\{a, -a\}$, we obtain $y_{ij}^k \leq z_{ij}^k, -y_{ij}^k \leq z_{ij}^k$. Similarly, the transformation $\bar{p}_{ij}^k - \bar{p}_{ij} = s_{ij}^k, \left|\bar{p}_{ij}^k - \bar{p}_{ij}\right| = t_{ij}^k$ yields $s_{ij}^k \leq t_{ij}^k, -s_{ij}^k \leq t_{ij}^k$. Using the above transformations, the last six constraints of the model (6.5) can be linearized. Subsequently, we replace the absolute value constraints as per above transformations to convert the nonlinear programming model (6.4) into an equivalent linear programming model (6.5). Furthermore, by solving the linear model (6.5), we can obtain optimal solution for the CMCC model (6.4).

For most existing MCC models, the unit adjustment cost of each expert is usually assumed to be precisely known. However, in practical decision-making problems, it is very difficult for the moderator to determine the exact values for such costs. Furthermore, since experts involved in GDM usually come from various social groups, they have different social experiences and represent distinct interests, which implies that the corresponding unit adjustment cost may be uncertain. Therefore, below we developed a robust CMCC model for MCGDM with uncertain costs, which allows for minimizing the worst-case total compensation cost and enhancing the stability of the model solution.

Classical MCC models assume that the costs of modifying experts' opinions are fixed crisp values. However, in the robust consensus problem, the only information available regarding the uncertain unit adjustment costs c_k is that they belong to an uncertainty set $\mathcal{U}$. So, the cost function in the robust form of the model (6.4) is given as:

$$\sum_{k=1}^{K}\sum_{i=1}^{m}\sum_{j=1}^{n} c_k \left| \bar{p}_{ij}^k - p_{ij}^k \right|, c_k \in \mathcal{U}$$

Without any loss of generality, we can assume that each $c_k \in \mathcal{U}$ may be expressed as

$$c_k = c_k^0 + \xi_k \hat{c}_k, k = 1, 2, \ldots, K,$$

where c_k^0 is the nominal unit adjustment cost and $\hat{c}_k$ is the corresponding perturbation value. The uncertain parameter $\xi = (\xi_1, \ldots, \xi_K)$ belongs to a perturbation set $\mathcal{Z}$, which must be convex and closed, and controls the perturbation range of the uncertainty. Here, we will assume that the perturbation set is a budget uncertainty set, which is defined based on the maximum norm and the 1-norm. It can be mathematically expressed as:

$$\mathcal{Z}_\Gamma = \left\{ \xi \in \mathbb{R}^K : \| \xi \|_\infty \le 1, \| \xi \|_1 \le \Gamma \right\}$$

where $\Gamma \in [1, K]$ is known as the "uncertainty budget". The budget uncertainty set is essentially the intersection of two polytopes, and each point in the intersection may be related to a possible value of the uncertain unit cost. The next result determines the robust counterpart of the MC-CMCC models under the budget uncertainty set $\mathcal{Z}_\Gamma$. In other words, a robust version of model MC-CMCC can be defined as:

$$\min_{\left(\bar{p}_{ij}^k\right) \in \mathcal{M}([0,1])_{m \times n}} \sum_{k=1}^{K}\sum_{i=1}^{m}\sum_{j=1}^{n} c_k^0 \left| \bar{p}_{ij}^k - p_{ij}^k \right| + \sum_{k=1}^{K}\sum_{i=1}^{m}\sum_{j=1}^{n} \xi_k \hat{c}_k \left| \bar{p}_{ij}^k - p_{ij}^k \right|$$

$$s.t. \begin{cases} \xi_k \in \mathcal{Z}_\Gamma \\[2mm] \bar{p}_{ij} = \sum_{k=1}^{K} w_k \bar{p}_{ij}^k, i = 1, \ldots, m, j = 1, \ldots, n \\[2mm] \left| \bar{p}_{ij}^k - \bar{p}_{ij} \right| \le \varepsilon, k = 1, \ldots, K, i = 1, \ldots, m, j = 1, \ldots, n \\[2mm] 1 - \dfrac{1}{mn}\sum_{k=1}^{K}\sum_{i=1}^{m}\sum_{j=1}^{n} w_k \left| \bar{p}_{ij}^k - \bar{p}_{ij} \right| \ge \alpha \\[2mm] \bar{p}_i^k = \sum_{j=1}^{n} \omega_j \bar{p}_{ij}^k, i = 1, \ldots, m, k = 1, \ldots, K \\[2mm] \bar{p}_i = \sum_{k=1}^{K} w_k \bar{p}_i^k, i = 1, \ldots, m \\[2mm] \left| \bar{p}_i^k - \bar{p}_i \right| \le \beta, i = 1, \ldots, m, k = 1, \ldots, K \end{cases} \qquad (6.6)$$

The next result provides an equivalent version of the previous model that facilitates its resolution:

Theorem 2

Model (6.7) is a robust counterpart of model (6.4).

$$\min_{\left(\bar{p}_{ij}^k\right)\in\mathcal{M}([0,1])_{m\times n}} \sum_{k=1}^{K}\sum_{i=1}^{m}\sum_{j=1}^{n}c_k^0\left|\bar{p}_{ij}^k-p_{ij}^k\right|+\sum_{k=1}^{K}\left|u_k\right|+\tilde{A}\cdot\max_{k\in[1,K]\cap\mathbb{N}}\left|v_k\right|$$

$$s.t.\begin{cases}\sum_{i=1}^{m}\sum_{j=1}^{n}\hat{c}_k\left|\bar{p}_{ij}^k-p_{ij}^k\right|=-u_k-v_k,k=1,\dots,K\\[2mm]\bar{p}_{ij}=\sum_{k=1}^{K}w_k\bar{p}_{ij}^k,i=1,\dots,m,j=1,\dots,n\\[2mm]\left|\bar{p}_{ij}^k-\bar{p}_{ij}\right|\leq\varepsilon,k=1,\dots,K,i=1,\dots,m,j=1,\dots,n\\[2mm]1-\dfrac{1}{mn}\sum_{k=1}^{K}\sum_{i=1}^{m}\sum_{j=1}^{n}w_k\left|\bar{p}_{ij}^k-\bar{p}_{ij}\right|\geq\alpha\\[2mm]\bar{p}_i^k=\sum_{j=1}^{n}\omega_j\bar{p}_{ij}^k,i=1,\dots,m,k=1,\dots,K\\[2mm]\bar{p}_i=\sum_{k=1}^{K}w_k\bar{p}_i^k,i=1,\dots,m\\[2mm]\left|\bar{p}_i^k-\bar{p}_i\right|\leq\beta,i=1,\dots,m,k=1,\dots,K\end{cases}$$

(6.7)

Proof: Note that the perturbation set may be expressed as the intersection of two cones:

$$\mathcal{Z}=\left\{\xi\in\mathbb{R}^K:G_1\xi+g_1\in\mathcal{K}^1,G_2\xi+g_2\in\mathcal{K}^2\right\},$$

where

$$G_1\xi:=(\xi,0),g_1:=(0_{K\times1},1)\in\mathbb{R}^{K+1},G_2\xi:=(\xi,0),g_2:=(0_{K\times1},\Gamma)\in\mathbb{R}^{K+1},$$
$$\mathcal{K}^1=\left\{(h_1,h_2)\in\mathbb{R}^K\times\mathbb{R}:\|h_1\|_\infty\leq h_2\right\},\mathcal{K}^2=\left\{(h_1,h_2)\in\mathbb{R}^K\times\mathbb{R}:\|h_1\|_1\leq h_2\right\}.$$

Let us define $r_1:=(u,\tau_1)\in\mathcal{K}^2,r_2:=(v,\tau_2)\in\mathcal{K}^1$, where τ_1, τ_2 are non-negative numbers and u, $v\in\mathbb{R}^K$. Since $\mathcal{K}^1$ and $\mathcal{K}^2$ are dual cones, that is, $\mathcal{K}_*^1=\mathcal{K}^2,\mathcal{K}_*^2=\mathcal{K}^1$, according to the cone duality theory by Ben-Tal et al. (2009), the model R-MC-CMCC:1 is equivalent to:

$$\min_{(\bar{p}_{ij}^k)\in\mathcal{M}([0,1])_{m\times n}} B$$

$$s.t. \begin{cases} \displaystyle\sum_{k=1}^{K}\sum_{i=1}^{m}\sum_{j=1}^{n}c_k^0\left|\bar{p}_{ij}^k - p_{ij}^k\right| + \tau_1 + \Gamma\cdot\tau_2 \leq B \\[2ex] \displaystyle\sum_{i=1}^{m}\sum_{j=1}^{n}\hat{c}_k\left|\bar{p}_{ij}^k - p_{ij}^k\right| = -u_k - v_k, k = 1,\ldots,K \\[2ex] \|u\|_1 \leq \tau_1 \\[1ex] \|v\|_\infty \leq \tau_2 \\[1ex] \displaystyle\bar{p}_{ij} = \sum_{k=1}^{K}w_k\bar{p}_{ij}^k, i = 1,\ldots,m, j = 1,\ldots,n \\[2ex] \left|\bar{p}_{ij}^k - \bar{p}_{ij}\right| \leq \varepsilon, k = 1,\ldots,K, i = 1,\ldots,m, j = 1,\ldots,n \\[2ex] 1 - \displaystyle\frac{1}{mn}\sum_{k=1}^{K}\sum_{i=1}^{m}\sum_{j=1}^{n}w_k\left|\bar{p}_{ij}^k - \bar{p}_{ij}\right| \geq \alpha \\[2ex] \displaystyle\bar{p}_i^k = \sum_{j=1}^{n}\omega_j\bar{p}_{ij}^k, i = 1,\ldots,m, k = 1,\ldots,K \\[2ex] \displaystyle\bar{p}_i = \sum_{k=1}^{K}w_k\bar{p}_i^k, i = 1,\ldots,m \\[2ex] \left|\bar{p}_i^k - \bar{p}_i\right| \leq \beta, i = 1,\ldots,m, k = 1,\ldots,K \end{cases}$$

which is equivalent to (6.7).

Compared to model (6.4), the robust model (6.7) considers all possible values of unit adjustment cost in the uncertainty set and minimizes the minimum cost under worst-case scenarios, ensuring that the solution of the model is feasible for all uncertain scenarios. In contrast, model (6.4) only considers the compensation costs of the nominal scenario. Although it requires fewer compensation costs, it cannot handle data perturbations caused by external factors. This can lead to catastrophic losses in some practical decisions. For example, in some emergency decision-making problems, over-optimistic decisions that do not consider uncertainty may even threaten people's lives (Chakrabarti, 2021).

Theorem 3

Model (6.7) is equivalent to the linear robust model (6.8).

$$\min_{(\bar{p}_{ij}^k)\in\mathcal{M}([0,1])_{m\times n}} \sum_{k=1}^{K}\sum_{i=1}^{m}\sum_{j=1}^{n} c_k^0 z_{ij}^k + \sum_{k=1}^{K} \hat{u}_k + \Gamma \cdot V$$

$$s.t.\begin{cases} \sum_{i=1}^{m}\sum_{j=1}^{n} \hat{c}_k z_{ij}^k = -u_k - v_k, k = 1,\ldots,K \\[2mm] u_k \le \hat{u}_k, k = 1,\ldots,K \\ -u_k \le \hat{u}_k, k = 1,\ldots,K \\ v_k \le \hat{v}_k, k = 1,\ldots,K \\ -v_k \le \hat{v}_k, k = 1,\ldots,K \\ \hat{v}_k \le V, k = 1,\ldots,K \\ V \ge 0 \\[2mm] \bar{p}_{ij} = \sum_{k=1}^{K} w_k \bar{p}_{ij}^k, i = 1,\ldots,m, j = 1,\ldots,n \\[2mm] 1 - \frac{1}{mn}\sum_{k=1}^{K}\sum_{i=1}^{m}\sum_{j=1}^{n} w_k t_{ij}^k \ge \alpha \\[2mm] t_{ij}^k \le \varepsilon, k = 1,\ldots,K, i = 1,\ldots,m, j = 1,\ldots,n \\[2mm] \bar{p}_i^k = \sum_{j=1}^{n} \omega_j \bar{p}_{ij}^k, i = 1,\ldots,m, k = 1,\ldots,K \\[2mm] \bar{p}_i = \sum_{k=1}^{K} w_k \bar{p}_i^k, i = 1,\ldots,m \\[2mm] \bar{p}_{ij}^k - p_{ij}^k = y_{ij}^k, k = 1,\ldots,K, i = 1,\ldots,m, j = 1,\ldots,n \\ y_{ij}^k \le z_{ij}^k, k = 1,\ldots,K, i = 1,\ldots,m, j = 1,\ldots,n \\ -y_{ij}^k \le z_{ij}^k, k = 1,\ldots,K, i = 1,\ldots,m, j = 1,\ldots,n \\ \bar{p}_{ij}^k - \bar{p}_{ij} = s_{ij}^k, k = 1,\ldots,K, i = 1,\ldots,m, j = 1,\ldots,n \\ s_{ij}^k \le t_{ij}^k, k = 1,\ldots,K, i = 1,\ldots,m, j = 1,\ldots,n \\ -s_{ij}^k \le t_{ij}^k, k = 1,\ldots,K, i = 1,\ldots,m, j = 1,\ldots,n \\ \bar{p}_i^k - \bar{p}_i \le \beta, i = 1,\ldots,m, k = 1,\ldots,K \\ -\bar{p}_i^k + \bar{p}_i \le \beta, i = 1,\ldots,m, k = 1,\ldots,K \end{cases}$$

(6.8)

The proof process is similar to Theorem 1, and we will not describe it in detail for the sake of the brevity of this chapter. By solving the model (6.7), the optimal consensus preference $\bar{P}^1,\ldots,\bar{P}^K$ and the total compensation cost can be obtained.

6.4   CASE STUDY

This section provides an illustrative example of IoT platform selection to demonstrate the implementation process of the proposed approach. Then, a sensitivity analysis considering different parameters of the model (6.7) and consensus thresholds is performed.

6.4.1 Numerical Experiment

The cognitive Internet enables the intelligence of home appliances (Pramanik, Pal, & Choudhury, 2018). In this direction, commercial companies are working to update their devices and make them smarter to enhance market competitiveness. For example, Whirlpool is manufacturing smart washing machines that can be controlled by mobile devices (Kim & Moon, 2022). Xiaomi has launched an air purifier that can be operated remotely from a mobile phone and developed a smart module that can be integrated into all home appliances (Abdullah, Roobashini, & Alkawaz, 2021). With the development of IoT, smart home appliances will have greater cognition to assist users by detecting their intentions and usage patterns.

To improve market competitiveness, the company EasyTV wants to develop a new smart appliance that could perfectly cater to market demand. Therefore, EasyTV's CEOs need to choose which one of the most widely used IoT Platforms (Chakraborty et al., 2021; Kondratenko, Kondratenko, & Sidenko, 2018), namely Amazon Web Services (AWS), Google Cloud Platform, Microsoft Azure, Digital Ocean and IBM Watson IoT Platform, is the most suitable for the company. The evaluation criteria include device management, integration level, security and reliability levels, data collection protocols, variety of data analytics and database functionality (Kondratenko et al., 2018). To select the best IoT platform, EasyTV's CEOs will apply the proposed framework to make the final decision by asking the seven members of the advisory council. Table 6.1 shows the preference matrices provided by the seven experts, and the relevant parameter settings are shown in Table 6.2.

If no CRP is developed and the WA operator is directly used to fuse experts' preferences, the collective opinion is as follows:

$$P = \begin{bmatrix} 0.62 & 0.41 & 0.52 & 0.34 & 0.52 & 0.58 \\ 0.42 & 0.55 & 0.71 & 0.64 & 0.41 & 0.4 \\ 0.4 & 0.21 & 0.5 & 0.37 & 0.16 & 0.4 \\ 0.48 & 0.53 & 0.58 & 0.5 & 0.5 & 0.44 \\ 0.35 & 0.53 & 0.4 & 0.59 & 0.52 & 0.52 \end{bmatrix}$$

For this collective opinion, the consensus degree is $\mathbb{C}\left(P^1, P^2, \ldots, P^K\right)$ $= 1 - \sum_{k=1}^{K} w_k \left| P_k - P \right| = 0.765 \leq \alpha = 0.8$. And the maximum distance between experts' preferences and collective opinion for each alternative is $\left| p_3^2 - p_3 \right| = 0.355$. Since the experts are required to reach an agreed decision for a consensus degree greater than $\alpha = 0.8$ and the distance of the alternative's score need to be lower than $\beta = 0.1$, it is necessary to apply a robust CMCC model to adjust the experts' preferences, so as to improve the consensus degree. Taking the preferences in Table 6.1 and the parameters in Table 6.2 as input to the model (6.7), the optimal adjusted collective preference is

TABLE 6.1

Experts' Initial Preference Matrix

$$
P^1 = \begin{bmatrix}
0.63 & 0.55 & 0.16 & 0.01 & 0.33 & 0.9 \\
0.71 & 0.77 & 0.95 & 0.85 & 0.71 & 0.52 \\
0.42 & 0.18 & 0.87 & 0.16 & 0.19 & 0.94 \\
0.36 & 0.13 & 0.16 & 0.18 & 0.5 & 0.16 \\
0.49 & 0.69 & 0.49 & 0.46 & 0.78 & 0.87
\end{bmatrix}
\quad
P^2 = \begin{bmatrix}
0.45 & 0.77 & 0.05 & 0.57 & 0.94 & 0.1 \\
0.76 & 0.53 & 0.77 & 0.91 & 0.54 & 0.55 \\
0.91 & 0.6 & 0.95 & 0.69 & 0.19 & 0.65 \\
0.3 & 0.58 & 0.4 & 0.06 & 0.69 & 0.95 \\
0.04 & 0.04 & 0.72 & 0.82 & 0.21 & 0.45
\end{bmatrix}
$$

$$
P^3 = \begin{bmatrix}
0.28 & 0.23 & 0.18 & 0.04 & 0.46 & 0.62 \\
0.79 & 0.93 & 0.86 & 0.03 & 0.4 & 0.17 \\
0.27 & 0.43 & 0.65 & 0.27 & 0.31 & 0.46 \\
0.67 & 0.56 & 0.91 & 0.96 & 0.45 & 0.26 \\
0.23 & 0.54 & 0.01 & 0.76 & 0.68 & 0.41
\end{bmatrix}
\quad
P^4 = \begin{bmatrix}
0.76 & 0.05 & 0.76 & 0.28 & 0.82 & 0.81 \\
0.22 & 0.99 & 0.14 & 0.44 & 0.29 & 0.62 \\
0.54 & 0.06 & 0.42 & 0.25 & 0.01 & 0.14 \\
0.19 & 0.76 & 0.88 & 0.6 & 0.24 & 0.81 \\
0.73 & 0.05 & 0.06 & 0.67 & 0.05 & 0.34
\end{bmatrix}
$$

$$
P^5 = \begin{bmatrix}
0.64 & 0.43 & 0.9 & 0.94 & 0.59 & 0.59 \\
0.06 & 0.09 & 0.89 & 0.97 & 0.22 & 0.06 \\
0.16 & 0.07 & 0.39 & 0.57 & 0.06 & 0.15 \\
0.87 & 0.91 & 0.54 & 0.4 & 0.83 & 0.15 \\
0.23 & 0.76 & 0.83 & 0.63 & 0.99 & 0.65
\end{bmatrix}
\quad
P^6 = \begin{bmatrix}
0.88 & 0.21 & 0.54 & 0.0 & 0.39 & 0.64 \\
0.21 & 0.3 & 0.48 & 0.06 & 0.6 & 0.71 \\
0.23 & 0.27 & 0.25 & 0.45 & 0.12 & 0.62 \\
0.84 & 0.19 & 0.8 & 0.94 & 0.33 & 0.07 \\
0.56 & 0.97 & 0.48 & 0.81 & 0.85 & 0.18
\end{bmatrix}
$$

$$
P^7 = \begin{bmatrix}
0.74 & 0.86 & 0.65 & 0.19 & 0.03 & 0.03 \\
0.45 & 0.01 & 0.92 & 0.99 & 0.43 & 0.55 \\
0.47 & 0.19 & 0.03 & 0.32 & 0.36 & 0.26 \\
0.09 & 0.11 & 0.26 & 0.34 & 0.38 & 0.74 \\
0.04 & 0.76 & 0.32 & 0.06 & 0.01 & 0.48
\end{bmatrix}
$$

TABLE 6.2

Parameter Settings

c^0	$\hat{c}$	Experts' Weights	Criteria' Weights	ε	α	β	Γ
$\left(c_1^0,\dots,c_7^0\right)$ $=(2,2,1,3,2,3,1)$	$\left(\hat{c}_1,\dots,\hat{c}_7\right) = (0.75,$ $0.17, 0.28, 0.84,$ $0.52, 0.44, 0.16)$	$(w_1, \dots, w_7) =$ $(0.15, 0.08, 0.16,$ $0.20, 0.22, 0.06,$ $0.13)$	$(\omega_1, \dots, \omega_6) =$ $(0.24, 0.1, 0.17,$ $0.28, 0.12, 0.09)$	0.3	0.8	0.1	3

$$
\bar{P} = \begin{bmatrix}
0.64 & 0.35 & 0.42 & 0.44 & 0.35 & 0.43 \\
0.53 & 0.18 & 0.56 & 0.53 & 0.55 & 0.73 \\
0.47 & 0.54 & 0.47 & 0.28 & 0.6 & 0.37 \\
0.44 & 0.63 & 0.53 & 0.41 & 0.13 & 0.5 \\
0.55 & 0.6 & 0.45 & 0.37 & 0.45 & 0.52
\end{bmatrix}
$$

which implies a minimum total cost (TC) for reaching the consensus equal to $TC = 31.53$. Then the optimal overall evaluation value of each IoT platform is: $\bar{p}_1 = 0.46, \bar{p}_2 = 0.52, \bar{p}_3 = 0.43, \bar{p}_4 = 0.43, \bar{p}_5 = 0.47$.

Thus the ranking of the five IoT platforms can be obtained: $a_2 > a_5 > a_1 > a_3 = a_4$. Therefore, the Google Cloud Platform is the best choice.

6.4.2 SENSITIVITY ANALYSIS

This section analyzes the impact of changes in different parameters on the consensus cost in the model (6.7).

Figure 6.2 shows the variation of the TC with respect to the uncertainty level parameter Γ. Since the number of experts is 7, according to the definition of the budget uncertainty set, we vary Γ from 0 to 7 with a stepsize of 0.5 assuming that the unit adjustment costs of all experts are uncertain. As shown in Figure 6.2, the TC increases as Γ increases. This is because the uncertainty level parameter Γ controls the size of the uncertainty set. When Γ increases, the perturbation range of uncertain parameters expands. Therefore, to ensure that all possible scenarios are considered, the TC of the worst-oriented R-MC-CMCC model also increases with the expansion of the uncertainty set. Furthermore, $\Gamma = 0$, dictates that the model does not take into account uncertainty, and in this scenario the result is more optimistic than the robust cost.

Next, we analyze the impact of the consensus thresholds at the criteria level (ε), alternatives level (β) and group level (α) on the TC. For different configurations of these parameters, we solve the model (6.7) to compute the TC, and the results are reported. Figure 6.3 shows the impact of the three thresholds on the TC. Figure 6.3 (a) illustrates the variation of the TC with thresholds ε and β for a fixed group consensus level $\alpha = 0.8$. We observe that when ε or β decreases, more experts are needed

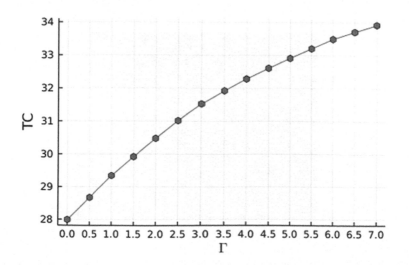

FIGURE 6.2 Variation of the total cost with respect to Γ.

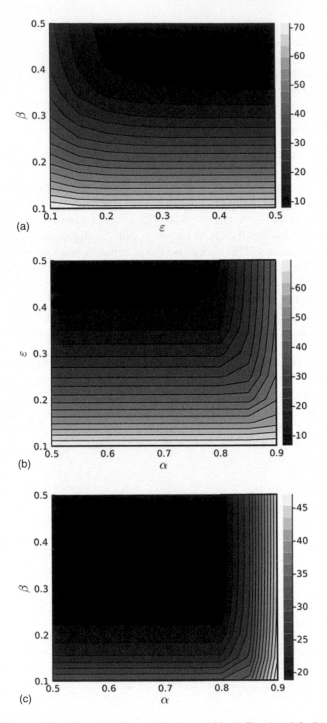

FIGURE 6.3 Total cost under different pairs of threshold. (a) Fixed α=0.8; (b) Fixed β=0.2; (c) Fixed ε=0.3.

to make changes, and the TC increases accordingly. When $\varepsilon < \beta$, alternative consensus level β does not have any effect on the model. Figure 6.3 (b) shows the variation of TC with criteria thresholds ε and consensus threshold α for $\beta = 0.2$. In this case, the TC decreases with an increasing ε and increases with an increasing α. This means that a higher consensus threshold drives more experts to make adjustments, resulting in higher consensus costs. And for larger ε, the consensus threshold α will have a stronger binding force on the consensus, thus increasing the consensus cost. Figure 6.3 (c) shows the variation of TC with the alternative level threshold β and consensus level α for a fixed $\varepsilon = 0.3$. A similar result to Figure 6.3 (b) can be obtained, where TC decreases with increasing alternative level threshold and increases with increasing consensus threshold. When $\beta > \varepsilon = 0.3$, the change of β will no longer affect the consensus cost, which further confirms the result of Figure 6.3 (a).

6.5 CONCLUSIONS

Nowadays, consensus decisions are increasingly important in MCGDM problems. To obtain a consensus solution agreed by the majority of experts, CRP is used to soften the disagreements among experts. Considering the calculation of consensus through different consensus measures, the CMCC model preserves as much as possible the experts' initial opinions while ensuring a desired group consensus degree. However, these CMCC models focus on single-criteria decision-making problems, and they may not be efficient for dealing with MCGDM problems. Furthermore, they do not take into account the uncertainty of the expert's unit adjustment cost, which is very common in real-world decision-making problems.

This chapter develops a new CMCC model for the MCGDM problem, which allows experts to express their preferences for alternatives based on multiple evaluation criteria, expressed in the form of a decision matrix. In addition to the classic constraints considered in CMCC models, the linear model (6.5) includes an additional restriction to guarantee consensus on the final decision that is made according to the weights of the criteria. Furthermore, in the model (6.4), in order to solve the uncertainty of the unit adjustment cost of experts, this chapter establishes the model (6.4) based on robust optimization, which increases the stability of the model. Finally, to demonstrate the usability and advantages of the proposed model (6.7), an illustrative example of the selection of an IoT platform and the corresponding sensitivity analysis was performed.

In future research, we will investigate the applicability and performance of different uncertainty sets (Han, Ji & Qu, 2021), extend the proposed multi-criteria CMCC models to large-scale MCGDM problems (García-Zamora, Labella, Ding, Rodríguez & Martínez, 2022b) and deeper analyze the relation between the parameters involved in the model (García-Zamora, Dutta, Massanet, Riera & Martínez, 2022a).

ACKNOWLEDGMENTS

This work is partially supported by the Spanish Ministry of Economy and Competitiveness through the Spanish National Project PGC2018-099402-B-I00, the FEDER-UJA project 1380637 and ERDF, the Spanish Ministry of Science, Innovation and Universities through a Formación de Profesorado Universitario (FPU2019/01203) grant, the Junta de Andalucía Andalusian Plan for Research, Development and Innovation (POSTDOC 21-00461) and the Grants for the Requalification of the Spanish University System for 2021–2023 in the María Zambrano modality (UJA13MZ).

REFERENCES

Abdullah, M.I., Roobashini, D., & Alkawaz, M.H. (2021). Active monitoring of energy utilization in smart home appliances. *2021 IEEE 11th IEEE symposium on computer applications & industrial electronics (ISCAIE)* (pp. 245–249). doi: 10.1109/ISCAIE51753.2021.9431776

Ben-Arieh, D., & Easton, T. (2007). Multi-criteria group consensus under linear cost opinion elasticity. *Decision Support Systems, 43* (3), 713–721.

Ben-Tal, A., El Ghaoui, L., & Nemirovski, A. (2009). *Robust optimization* (Vol. 28). Princeton, New Jersey: Princeton University Press.

Büyüközkan, G., & Güleryüz, S. (2016). A new integrated intuitionistic fuzzy group decision making approach for product development partner selection. *Computers & Industrial Engineering, 102*, 383–395.

Chakrabarti, D. (2021). Parameter-free robust optimization for the maximum-sharpe portfolio problem. *European Journal of Operational Research, 293* (1), 388–399.

Chakraborty, A., Jindal, M., Khosravi, M.R., Singh, P., Shankar, A., & Diwakar, M. (2021). A secure IoT-based cloud platform selection using entropy distance approach and fuzzy set theory. *Wireless Communications and Mobile Computing, 2021*, 1–11.

Dong, Y., Xu, Y., Li, H., & Feng, B. (2010). The OWA-based consensus operator under linguistic representation models using position indexes. *European Journal of Operational Research, 203* (2), 455–463.

Fedrizzi, M., Fedrizzi, M., & Pereira, R.A.M. (1999). Soft consensus and network dynamics in group decision making. *International Journal of Intelligent Systems, 14* (1), 63–77.

Fu, C., Chang, W., & Yang, S. (2020). Multiple criteria group decision making based on group satisfaction. *Information Sciences, 518*, 309–329.

García-Zamora, D., Dutta, B., Massanet, S., Riera, J.V., Martínez, L. (2022a). Relationship between the distance consensus and the consensus degree in comprehensive minimum cost consensus models: A polytope-based analysis. *European Journal of Operational Research.* doi: 10.1016/j.ejor.2022.08.015

García-Zamora, D., Labella, Á., Ding, W., Rodríguez, R.M., & Martínez, L. (2022b, Jun). Large-scale group decision making: A systematic review and a critical analysis. *IEEE/CAA Journal of Automatica Sinica, 9* (6), 949–966.

Gong, Z., Zhang, H., Forrest, J., Li, L., Xu, X. (2015). Two consensus models based on the minimum cost and maximum return regarding either all individuals or one individual. *European Journal of Operational Research, 240* (1), 183–192.

Han, Y., Ji, Y., Qu, S. (2021). A robust minimum-cost consensus model with uncertain aggregation weights based on data-driven method. *IEEE Transactions on Computational Social Systems, 9* (4), 1167–1184.

Han, Y., Qu, S., Wu, Z., Huang, R. (2019). Robust consensus models based on minimum cost with an application to marketing plan. *Journal of Intelligent & Fuzzy Systems, 37* (4), 5655–5668.

Kacprzyk, J. (1986). Group decision making with a fuzzy linguistic majority. *Fuzzy Sets and Systems, 18* (2), 105–118.

Kim, S., & Moon, H. (2022). Understanding consumer acceptance of smart washing machines: How do female consumers' occupations affect the acceptance process? *International Journal of Human–Computer Interaction*, 1–22. doi: 10.1080/10447318.2022.2049135

Kondratenko, Y., & Kondratenko, G., Sidenko, I. (2018). Multi-criteria decision making for selecting a rational IoT platform. *2018 IEEE 9th international conference on dependable systems, services and technologies (dessert)* (pp. 147–152). doi: 10.1109/DESSERT.2018.8409117

Kuhn, D., Esfahani, P.M., Nguyen, V.A., & Shafieezadeh-Abadeh, S. (2019). Wasserstein distributionally robust optimization: Theory and applications in machine learning. In *Operations research & management science in the age of analytics* (pp. 130–166). Washington: Informs.

Labella, Á., Liu, H., & Rodríguez, R.M., Martínez, L. (2020). A cost consensus metric for consensus reaching processes based on a comprehensive minimum cost model. *European Journal of Operational Research, 281* (2), 316–331.

Li, Y., Zhang, H., & Dong, Y. (2017). The interactive consensus reaching process with the minimum and uncertain cost in group decision making. *Applied Soft Computing, 60,* 202–212.

Nie, R.-X., Tian, Z.-P., & Wang, J.-Q., Luo, H.-Y. (2020). An objective and interactive-information-based feedback mechanism for the consensus-reaching process considering a non-support degree for minority opinions. *Expert Systems, 37* (5), e12543.

Palomares, I., Estrella, F.J., Martínez, L., & Herrera, F. (2014). Consensus under a fuzzy context: Taxonomy, analysis framework AFRYCA and experimental case of study. *Information Fusion, 20,* 252–271.

Palomares, I., Martinez, L., & Herrera, F. (2013). A consensus model to detect and manage noncooperative behaviors in large-scale group decision making. *IEEE Transactions on Fuzzy Systems, 22* (3), 516–530.

Pramanik, P.K.D., Pal, S., & Choudhury, P. (2018). Beyond automation: The cognitive IoT. Artificial intelligence brings sense to the internet of things. *Cognitive computing for big data systems over IoT* (pp. 1–37). Cham: Springer.

Qin, J., Liu, X., & Pedrycz, W. (2017). An extended TODIM multi-criteria group decision making method for green supplier selection in interval type-2 fuzzy environment. *European Journal of Operational Research, 258* (2), 626–638.

Qu, S., Han, Y., Wu, Z., & Raza, H. (2021). Consensus modeling with asymmetric cost based on data-driven robust optimization. *Group Decision and Negotiation, 30* (6), 1395–1432.

Rodríguez, R.M., Labella, Á., & De Tré, G., Martínez, L. (2018). A large scale consensus reaching process managing group hesitation. *Knowledge-Based Systems, 159,* 86–97.

Rodríguez, R.M., Labella, Á., & Dutta, B., Martínez, L. (2021). Comprehensive minimum cost models for large scale group decision making with consistent fuzzy preference relations. *Knowledge-Based Systems, 215,* 106780.

Roubens, M. (1997). Fuzzy sets and decision analysis. *Fuzzy sets and systems, 90* (2), 199–206.

Tian, Z.-P., Nie, R.-X., Wang, J.-Q., Long, R.-Y. (2020). Adaptive consensus-based model for heterogeneous large-scale group decision-making: detecting and managing noncooperative behaviors. *IEEE Transactions on Fuzzy Systems, 29* (8), 2209–2223.

Wu, Z., & Xu, J. (2016). Managing consistency and consensus in group decision making with hesitant fuzzy linguistic preference relations. *Omega, 65,* 28–40.

Xu, X., Yin, X., & Chen, X. (2019). A large-group emergency risk decision method based on data mining of public attribute preferences. *Knowledge-Based Systems, 163,* 495–509.

Xu, X.-H., Du, Z.-J., & Chen, X.-H. (2015). Consensus model for multi-criteria large-group emergency decision making considering non-cooperative behaviors and minority opinions. *Decision Support Systems, 79,* 150–160.

Zhang, B., Dong, Y., & Xu, Y. (2013). Maximum expert consensus models with linear cost function and aggregation operators. *Computers & Industrial Engineering, 66* (1), 147–157.

Zhang, B., Liang, H., Gao, Y., & Zhang, G. (2018). The optimization-based aggregation and consensus with minimum-cost in group decision making under incomplete linguistic distribution context. *Knowledge-Based Systems, 162,* 92–102.

Zhang, G., Dong, Y., Xu, Y., & Li, H. (2011). Minimum-cost consensus models under aggregation operators. *IEEE Transactions on Systems, Man, and Cybernetics-Part A: Systems and Humans, 41* (6), 1253–1261.

Zhang, H., Kou, G., & Peng, Y. (2019). Soft consensus cost models for group decision making and economic interpretations. *European Journal of Operational Research, 277* (3), 964–980.

Zhang, N., Gong, Z., & Chiclana, F. (2017). Minimum cost consensus models based on random opinions. *Expert Systems with Applications, 89*, 149–159.

Zhong, X., Xu, X., & Pan, B. (2022). A non-threshold consensus model based on the minimum cost and maximum consensus-increasing for multi-attribute large group decision-making. *Information Fusion, 77*, 90–106.

Index

Pages in *italics* refer to figures and pages in **bold** refer to tables.

110   Index

DimProduct, *see* under tables
DimStore, *see* under tables
Directed Acyclic Graph, *see* DAG
dominance degree-based ranking, 72
DNN, 53
dunnhumby, 30

E

electric car, *see* NEV
ELICIT
    aggregation operator for, 9
    Choquet-OWA operator, 9, *13*
    expressions of, **17**
    information, 2–4, 8, 12, *13*, 18
emissions trading schemes, *see* ETS
Enterprise architecture frameworks, 42
entropy, 66–67, 69–70, 73, 75–76, 82, **83**, 85
Environmental, Social and Governance, *see* ESG
ER, 67, 85
    algorithm, 70–71, 73
    information fusion approach, 76
ESG, 38, **40**, **45**, 49
    application layer, 46, 48
    data architecture, 42
    data collection layer, 44–45, 48
    data lifecycle, 39, 42, 44
    data processing layer, 45, 48
    data processing requirements for, 44
    data quality issues, 43
    DevOps, 43, 46
    emerging activities of, 39
    initiatives, 39, **40**
    IT considerations, 44
    models, *41*, 42
    research challenges, 38, *41*
    situation-specific design, 43
    software design for, 44, 49
    stakeholders and, 43, 45
    systems, 48
ETL, 21; *see also* data pipeline
ETS, 47
Evidential Reasoning, *see* ER
extract, transform, load, *see* ETL

F

FactSale, *see* under tables
feature engineering, 22
Feature Pipelines, *22*, *24*, *26*, 35
FLA, 1–2, 66
FM1 processing graph, *30*
fuzzy decisions
    type 2, 67–68, *69*, 73, 75; *see also* FLA
fuzzy linguistic approach, *see* FLA
fuzzy measure, Sugeno's, 7
fuzzy preference relationship-based ranking, 72

G

gated recurrent unit, *see* GRU
GDM, 90, 96; *see also* MCGDM
GHG, 45–46, 48–49
Global Reporting Standards, *see* GRI
GPipe
    module, 32
    process flow, *25*, *32*
greenhouse gas emissions, *see* GHG
GRI, **40**
group decision making, *see* GDM
GRU, 53–55, 58–59
    accuracy rates, *62*
    deep learning methods, 60; *see also* deep
        learning

H

hesitant fuzzy linguistic term sets, *see* HFLTS
HFLTS, 2
home appliances, 101
human activity, 1
hyper-parameters configuration, **60**

I

IASB, **40**
IFRS, **40**
ignorant sentiment, 74
ILP, **40**
International Accounting Standards Board, *see*
    IASB
International Financial Reporting Standard, *see*
    IFRS
International Sustainability Standards Board, *see*
    ISSB
internet of things, *see* IoT
internet reviews, *see* OTR
Investment Leadership Program, *see* ILP
IoT, 46, *47*, 101
    application development, 43
    devices, 45, 47
    platform selection, 90, 100–105
    reference frameworks, 42
ISSB, **40**
IT2FS, 66–69, 73, 75, 82

K

Kafka, 23, *25*

L

language independent sentiment analysis, *see* LISA
LDA, 66–67
Linguistic distributed information, **82–83**